D1647681

To: R

What is wrong is
wrong even if everyone
is doing it.

4/16/15

ALSO BY AARON BEAM:

HEALTHSOUTH: THE WAGON TO DISASTER

with Chris Warner

ETHICS PLAYBOOK: WINNING ETHICALLY IN BUSINESS

AARON BEAM
WITH GREG WOMBLE

Copyright 2015 Aaron Beam

All rights reserved. No part of this book may be used or re-produced by any means, graphic, electronic, or mechanical, including photocopying, recording, taping or by any information storage retrieval system without the written permission of the author except in the case of brief quotations embodied in critical articles and reviews.

Because of the dynamic nature of the Internet, any Web addresses or links contained in this book may have changed since publication and may no longer be valid.

Cartoon on page 83 used by permission. Robert Weber/The New Yorker Collection/The Cartoon Bank

For information about the author, speaking engagement booking or bulk book sales, visit aaronbeam.net.

DEDICATION

To Father Paul Zoghby and Cordy Drollinger

On Easter Sunday of 2012, I became a member of St. Margaret of Scotland Catholic Church in Robertsdale, Alabama. Two people played a big role in my decision: Father Paul Zoghby and parishioner Cordy Drollinger. Father Zoghby's RCIA classes lead me to my decision and Cordy, in her wonderful accent, encouraged me to join the church. The Holy Spirit told me this lady knew what she was saying.

I am sure the Holy Spirit was guiding me as I wrote this book. I also feel confident that the merging of my journeys to become a more ethical person and to become a Christian was no coincidence.

Thank you, Father. Thank you, Cordy.

CONTENTS

ACKNOWLEDGEMENTS

I want to thank those whom I interviewed for this book. They were very generous with their time and knowledge: Marianne Jennings, Dr. Dan Ariely, Dr. Leslie Sekerka, Dr. Linda Trevino, Buddy Roemer, Eric Fink, Sarah Polhill, Guinn Massey, and Deborah Lawson.

Since 2009, I have been asked by many college professors to speak to their classes. While these individuals were not interviewed specifically for the book, they did have a big influence on my writing. Often they would take me to lunch or dinner and we discussed ethical issues. I have spent the most time with Barbara Danos at LSU. My third speech was to her class and since then, I have spoken to her students over a dozen times. Her feedback and encouraging remarks after my presentations have been an important catalyst for writing this book. All of the professors that have asked me to return for multiple visits have had a big impact on me. In this group are Dr. Megan Hess of Washington and Lee University, Dr. Paul Melendez of University of Arizona, Dr. Mark Lehman of Mississippi State University, Sarah Stanwick of Auburn University, Jennifer Kish-Gephart of University of Arkansas, Dr. Jacquelyn Moffitt of LSU, Dr. Todd DeZoort of University of Alabama, Dr. Peter Ricchiuti of Tulane University, Dr. J. Richard Dietrich of Ohio State University, Dr. Mark Wilder of University of Mississippi, Dr. Brad Shrader of Iowa State University, and Dr. Clark Wheatley of Florida International University.

I would like to thank Healthcare Financial Managers Association, Alabama State Bar, AICPA, IMA, ACFE, various state hospital associations, and many state CPA associations.

I am grateful for the individuals who have assisted me with this project, including Nancy Womble, Joe Walker, Chris Warner, Walter Pavlo, Dr. David Larcker, Weston Smith, Wade

Kirkpatrick, Denise O'Brien, and Dr. Ed Watson.

I would like to especially thank three people: Marianne Jennings, Dan Ariely, and my wife, Phyllis. Before I ever started writing the book I explained the concept to Dr. Jennings. She assured me that the concept had merit and that she would like to contribute in some way. I started writing the book the next day.

Dr. Ariely's research in the area of ethics influenced my writing more than any other person. His willingness to help was more than I ever expected. I'm reminded of a quote from Richard Branson: "Complexity is your enemy. Any fool can make something complicated. It is hard to make something simple." Dr. Ariely's true genius is that he can make complex issues very simple to understand.

Without a doubt, Professor Jennings and Dr. Ariely are leaders in the field of ethics education and I am indebted to them for their contribution to this book.

Thanks to Phyllis for her support in this project, especially for transcribing my terrible handwriting. Her feedback on my writing was very valuable.

I was able to partially fund the cost of this book through a Kickstarter campaign. I would like to thank those who provided financial backing for this project:

Dan Ariely
Donald Briskman
Connie Brown
Lucy Buffett
Sharon Cain
Meredith Calhoun
Rick Carter
Don Chance
Cecil Christenberry
Thomas Coghlan
Denise Cook
Tim and Cathie Corrigan
Bruce Cozadd
Robert Cunningham
Barbara Danos
Brian Dearing
Philip Dembowski
David Dingler
Cordy Drollinger
Hays and Carolyn Dunnam
Victoria Estopinal
Andrea Frankle
Brigitte Fredy
Andrew Freeman
Nicole and Chip Gaillard
Albert Gauthreaux
Dan Gibson
Don Goldzband
Keith and Marie Guillot
Barry Hair
Seth Hargett
Dewayne Hayes

Tammy Hermann
Megan Hess
Marianne Jennings
Carol and Glen Jesse
John Karl
Jenny Klein
Deborah Lawson
Russell Ledbetter
Mark Lehman
Amanda Lemay
Albert Lugo
Mac McAleer
Colleen McNorton
Yael Melamede
Andy Millard
Walter Pavlo
Teresa and Don Rhodes
Peter Ricchiuti
John Rivenbark
Laura Roberts
Jack Schaeffer
Stanford Sewell
Susan Sims
Weston and Dee Smith
Macey Taylor
Danny and Lou Ann
    VanDeventer
Tommy Washington
Shanna and Wade Wilkins
Tom Williams
Greg and Nancy Womble
Rev. Paul Zoghby

I knew who Aaron Beam was long before we met. After the multi-billion dollar HealthSouth scandal, I studied the history of its fraudulent fall. Aaron was one of a long line of CFOs who had left the company prior to the collapse. The phenomenon of the revolving CFO door was something I had found in other firms that had experienced ethical collapses: Enron, Tyco, American Continental, and many others. The list had become far too long.

After the HealthSouth fraud, I was able to synthesize the research I had been gathering for 30 years on corporate ethical breakdowns for my book, *The Seven Signs of Ethical Collapse*. It presents the common threads in organizations that experience ethical collapse: financial issues, often fraud, and, always, headlines that engender disbelief as people ask, "How could they have gotten away with this for so long?" But the book was written to be forward-looking, and to help organizations know how to pick up those faint signals and realize they are vulnerable. My research, culminating with the HealthSouth story, taught me that ethical collapse can be prevented. The book even made a few predictions in the last chapters about companies that were at risk. Sadly, those predictions proved to be true. No one in them read the book.

As a result of writing that book, I met Aaron Beam. Colleagues who had heard Aaron speak told me that he pointed to my work and said, "She has it exactly right." Academics don't often get validation from original sources with experience. I was glad to have it, and felt privileged to meet Aaron at a conference. Following our introduction, we began to exchange emails. As a result, he has come to Arizona State University three times to speak to my students. When Aaron speaks, you can hear a pin drop on the carpeted floors of the graduate classrooms. Students sit mesmerized as this former CPA explains how easy it is to fall into the traps that lead to felonies.

After Aaron speaks, you know he has had an effect because the students will mention him throughout the remainder of the trimester. Aaron is a compelling figure whose story often scares the living daylights out of those who hear it. His story forces us to face the realization that those who land in ethical and legal difficulty in business are not always demons; sometimes they are decent folks who lose their way. His presentations explain how he lost his way, and describe the ordinariness of the first few tiny steps, seemingly innocuous, that then grew into fraud. That message demands introspection in students, professionals, and anyone else who works in organizational life.

When you hear Aaron speak, you hear a compelling story but you are also left wanting more. What you want is a resource manual, something you can turn to for checks and balances on your conduct. How do you know when you are slipping? What does a bad ethical culture look like? What do you do when no one is listening to your concerns? What does fraud look like at its inception?

Those who have heard Aaron speak encouraged him to write a handbook, something that would help them understand where those lines between "no big deal" and fraud begin. This is that book.

Aaron has done the introspection that guilty pleas and prison demand, but so few undertake. He knows exactly where those slipping points are and what to do when you reach them. He reached those points, succumbed, and realized too late that he was at the point of no return. We would rather not learn these ethical lessons the hard way, and, in *Ethics Playbook*, Aaron offers his experience, his reflections, and his earnest research to help us.

We owe a debt of gratitude to this man for being so willing

to open up and share with us. From the complex research of scholars to the wit and wisdom of the ages, Aaron offers us insight into the pressures, psychology, and culture that can grab us and pull us into ethical missteps. He then gives us the courage and conviction to not give in and run away from the conduct, the manager, and often, the company culture that tries to ensnare us.

This is not a book that simply tells a story of someone who made bad choices and the resulting consequences. This is a book that teaches and offers the wisdom of reflection that too few undertake after the experience of federal prison. You won't find Aaron's lessons in the fraud triangle or in the glib mantras of the moment. This is a book that charts new territory in asking all of us to proceed with caution when facing the turning points we may miss in our day-to-day demands—or because of the increasing rewards we receive for just going along. There is a strength in Aaron that comes through in his candor and willingness to share tender moments such as the impact of his actions on his family and the journey to his faith.

You will laugh, you will learn, and you will understand how easy it is to fall into these ethical traps. You will walk away with a desire to follow the advice Aaron offers. The man knows whereof he speaks.

Marianne Jennings, Professor Emeritus
W. P. Carey School of Business
Arizona State University

INTRODUCTION

I love college football. Especially LSU Tiger football. In fact, I built a full-sized football field at my former residence, Beam Acres, although to this day I'm not sure why. Maybe it was because I could.

I still live near the Alabama Gulf coast but not on a 25-acre estate with a football field, luxury cars in the garage, and the cash to vacation anywhere in the world. After losing nearly everything I had and going to prison for accounting fraud, I had some reflection to do. But I also had to make a living, so I started mowing other people's lawns while trying to figure out how my life got so out of whack.

How did I go from high-flier to felon? That's a story I tell in my first book, *HealthSouth: The Wagon to Disaster*. Here are the high points:

- In 1984, I became co-founder and founding Chief Financial Officer of HealthSouth, which revolutionized how physical therapy was delivered to post-operative patients, injured athletes, and others.
- The company went public just three years later and became one of the nation's largest healthcare companies.
- After a decade of amazing company growth, I followed the lead of our Chief Executive Officer, Richard Scrushy, and, in 1996, agreed to help cook the books to meet the aggressive quarterly earnings projections Wall Street expected.
- The following year, with a gnawing conscience that I tried to ease with alcohol, I retired from HealthSouth and soon relocated with my family to the Alabama Gulf coast.
- In 2003, a massive, $3 billion fraud was revealed at HealthSouth and the executive suite, including Scrushy, was wiped clean.

- I immediately told the FBI about my involvement and pled guilty for my participation. I became a key witness in criminal proceedings against my former CEO.
- Scrushy was charged on 36 counts, including fraud, money laundering and conspiracy charges.
- Scrushy was found not guilty on all counts.
- I paid restitution, was fined, and spent three months in a federal minimum-security prison.

Why I Wrote This Book

Every day I think about the wrong I did and the people I irreparably harmed. While rebuilding my life after prison, I came to realize that I needed to share my story with others so they could avoid making the same mistakes and committing the same crimes. After repeated suggestions from my wife, Phyllis, I gathered my courage, contacted the LSU business school, and asked if I could tell my story to their students. They agreed.

Since that first speaking engagement in 2009, I've shared my story with more than 250 audiences in corporate and associational meetings, university auditoriums, high school classrooms, and churches. I also speak to a lot of civic groups, auditing and accounting audiences, and healthcare-related groups. In my presentation I tell people about my ethical mistakes and encourage them to do better.

But becoming an author again? I was convinced that *The Wagon to Disaster* would be my last book. After all, my background was that of a bean counter, not a writer. What else did I have to say? HealthSouth had certainly cleaned up its act, and has again become a highly respected player on the national healthcare scene. And what about the rest of the business landscape? After scandals were revealed at WorldCom, Tyco, Exxon, Lehman, Fannie Mae and other organizations, hadn't there been measurable improvement in the ethical behavior of those in the American business world?

Unfortunately, even though I'm an optimist by nature, I have to say that we still have a long, long way to go in this country when it comes to doing business ethically. In fact, I've talked with some people who are convinced that the ship has sailed too far from shore to be brought back.

But I don't think so. I'm hopeful, and that's why I wrote this book.

It's for All of Us

When I first started speaking publicly, I focused only on telling my HealthSouth story. I soon realized, though, that my audiences wanted to know what they could personally do to prevent ethical lapses in the workplace. I noticed during Q and A sessions after my talks that certain questions were repeatedly asked.

This book addresses those questions in a practical way. It isn't just for CEOs or CFOs; it's for anybody who works in business or hopes to do so one day. It's for those who believe in operating within clear ethical boundaries but need some help recognizing them. It's written for those frustrated corporate employees who keep choosing toxic, numbers-only business cultures where the issue of "doing business right" never comes up in conversation. It's for young people who want to do well, but want to do right, too—and need a little encouragement that the deck isn't stacked against them as they start their career journey. This book is also for those of us who still believe in right and wrong and think that the American Dream becomes more meaningful and accessible to people when businesses operate in a fair and honest manner.

And finally, it's for all of us who understand that taking dishonest shortcuts, defrauding stockholders, hiding from regulators, making phony public statements, and cooking the books doesn't just result in disaster for the offending enterprise—it's a disaster for all of us. It crashes stocks. It drains retirement savings. It decreases trust in our institutions. And it swells the unemployment rolls.

You don't have to look very hard for examples. Just think about the subprime mortgage/banking debacle of a few years ago. That series of scandals changed the country for the worse in very tangible ways. We'll be recovering from it for years to come.

This isn't, however, the HealthSouth story, volume two. It's not a set of case study analyses or an academic book. There are some very smart experts that do a great job of that, and I quote a few of them in this book.

Rather, this little book is more of a playbook, a set of practical ideas and principles that you can use wherever you are and in whatever career stage you find yourself.

How the Book Breaks Down

Section One kicks off with a look at the environment of fraud. What does a fraudulent company look like and who are the players? How do they contribute to the fraud? You may be surprised by some of the answers.

Section Two looks at why we lie and cheat in the workplace—after all, we're good people, aren't we? We examine the role of emotions in fraud, the conflicts of interest that are pervasive in a fraudulent environment, and the shades of grey that make slipping into fraud so easy.

Section Three is a playbook for your personal business success. We look at starting ethics training early and developing the ethical muscle you need to thrive honestly in the workplace. After answering the question, "Is there an ethical core?" we'll discuss ways to find an ethical workplace and what to do if your dream job becomes an ethical nightmare.

In the final section, we discover ways companies and other organizations can build a culture that values the right things—not just the bottom line. We'll also find out why ethics education and business transparency are so important.

Throughout the book, I've included dozens of short Ethical Plays that you can absorb without taking a time-out from reading the book. Many of these ideas are found in my Ethical Playing Cards deck, which has become quite popular.

Back to Football

Which gets us back to football.

When I was in prison, there were two types of people: LSU fans and everybody else. Actually, the two basic types of prisoners were white-collar criminals like me and non-violent drug dealers. Most of them, it seemed, were from Miami.

Being a huge LSU fan, I couldn't wait for the 2005 match-up between my beloved Tigers and the Miami Hurricanes in the Peach Bowl. The night before the big game, three of the drug dealers approached me in the lobby as I was writing a letter. One of them ordered me to hand over my shoelaces, and I asked him why. After a long pause he said, "Because we don't want you to hang yourself when Miami beats LSU's ass tomorrow night!"

Well, the 40-3 stomping LSU put on the Hurricanes assured my fellow inmates that I was no suicide risk. In fact, I felt great. For a few minutes, as I watched that game, I could see clearly. Good and evil. There were no grey areas. It was like an old-fashioned Western movie: the good guys won.

I wish I could tell you that everything in business appears as black and white, with no grey areas. I can't. But the good guys (and gals) *can* win in business. It takes hard work, sharp senses to avoid ethical landmines, and more than a little courage.

I wish I had had that courage when it mattered most. Maybe you will. Maybe this book will help you.

PART ONE: THE GAME AND ITS PLAYERS

CHAPTER 1

What's New about Dishonesty?

Maybe something was in the water, but Birmingham, Alabama in the 1980s and 1990s sprouted several innovative and profitable companies. This list includes pre-fraud HealthSouth, of course, but also a chain of book superstores, a number of regional banks, and a company called Just For Feet.

South African entrepreneur Harold Ruttenberg developed a concept for an athletic-shoe superstore that included knowledgeable salespeople, brightly lit vendor displays, loud rock music, and a half-court basketball floor where customers would try out their shoe selection. The stores would also have giant video displays—still a novelty in 1988 when the larger-than-life Ruttenberg launched his first Just for Feet stores.

In 1992, the company went public. Then the domineering Ruttenberg chose his 29-year old son, Don-Allen Ruttenberg, as vice president for new store development. Seven years later, with sales of $775 million, Just for Feet was the nation's second-largest athletic shoe retailer with locations in 30 states.

But controversy followed father and son. After an accounting controversy involving store-opening costs, Wall Street took notice when Harold and his family sold large blocks of stock for almost $50 million.

Then in 1998, Don-Allen Ruttenberg created a fraudulent scheme to produce millions of dollars in fake income from the major athletic shoe vendors who had become cozy with top Just for Feet executives. Leveraging its massive buying power, Don-Allen persuaded the manufacturing executives to return false reports to Just for Feet's audit firm.

The house of cards started to fall. Cash flows were in the red, and, with a liquidity crisis looming, the company sold $200 million of high-yield junk bonds. Then they announced a first-ever quarterly loss, followed by default on its first interest payment on the junk bonds.

Before the end of the year, the company filed for Chapter 11 bankruptcy protection. This was followed by a flurry of investigations by state and local authorities including the FBI, SEC, and the U.S. Department of Justice. The company started asset liquidation under Chapter 7 of the U.S. bankruptcy code in early 2000, triggering lawsuits against the company's former executives and their auditor, Deloitte.

Several company executives pled guilty to criminal charges for their roles in the accounting fraud, including Don-Allen Ruttenberg. In 2005, a federal judge sentenced him to 20 months in prison and fined him $50,000. The senior Ruttenberg, who had long been retired from the CEO position and was gravely ill with cancer, was not charged in the case. Five executives from Just for Feet's former vendors also pleaded guilty for providing false confirmations to the company's auditors.

Deloitte received fines from the SEC and condemnation from the business media for the poor quality of its Just for Feet audits.

The New Theme

The theme of business people behaving badly isn't new. From unscrupulous used car dealers to phone sales scammers to retail bait-and-switchers—our cup runneth over with illustrations of the cheats and liars who earn our trust and then leave us holding the bag. And that bag doesn't always smell so good.

What is a relatively new theme in American life is the mega corporate fraud. Instead of creating negative impact for one or two consumers at a time, these larger, more strategic, and longer-lasting scams can rob thousands of investors and consumers of billions of dollars—not to mention their trust.

ETHICAL PLAY #1

"View ethics not as a deterrent but as an opportunity for success."

There are a lot of reasons why being ethical can help you be successful. The self-discipline that it takes to be ethical helps motivate you to make good choices. The respect you gain from others will build trust and open doors for you. There may be no greater measure of your character than the evidence that you are a person of your word.

Enron, WorldCom, HealthSouth, Tyco, Quest Communications; over the last 25 years the media has been full of stories that tell of good companies gone bad.

When fraud is systemic—such as the sub-prime mortgage debacle that started cracking wide open in 2008—it can not only ruin personal portfolios, but also destroy jobs, wound the U.S. economy, and wreck untold numbers of lives. And, yes, it also threatens the very public trust upon which our economy operates.

Why Do These Frauds Happen?

There's no simple answer to the question of why business fraud occurs. Even though I received a solid college education, served in the military and worked a couple of accounting jobs prior to joining HealthSouth in 1984, the phrase "business ethics" wasn't on my radar screen. I certainly didn't plan on doing anything illegal or unethical, although I saw questionable behavior by the CEO starting on the first day I met him.

Then, in 1996, I became a corporate fraudster. Even though I knew the numbers we reported were lies, I didn't speak out. I kept committing accounting fraud at HealthSouth until 1997 when I retired at the ripe old age of 54.

Had I planned it? No. Did I see it coming? If I'm honest (and I try to be) I have to say yes—but at this point in my life all I have is the rearview mirror and as we all know, that's much easier viewing.

Did Harold Ruttenberg plan for his incredible business vision to end in shame? Nobody does. Did he plan to reach the top of the sports shoe business by cheating his way there? I'm not a mind reader but I'm almost sure he didn't. Supercharged entrepreneurs and other high-performing business people are usually full of confidence, which means they have an attitude of being able to move mountains—if not single-handedly, then at least with the right, handpicked team—and having to cheat to get there probably isn't part of the original plan. They are opportunists but not con men, at least for the most part.

Who Is the Leader of the Pack?

In cases like Just for Feet and HealthSouth, there usually seems to be a larger-than-life, autocratic CEO at the center of the fraud. Often it's the founder, a guy with big dreams, endless confidence, and a lust for money. But is the CEO at the heart of every bad business model or corrupt organization?

No.

Even though frauds often start at the top, (the HealthSouth fraud started with a few simple words from the CEO, something that amounted to, "Fix this," which is ironic since from that moment, HealthSouth became a *broken* place), they also start in a hallway conversation between a manager and vendor. Or during a coffee break between board members. Or between employees who agree to hide the misdeeds of a co-worker.

Is there something in the water at these companies? Is unethical activity always the result of a rotten company culture or leadership's hubris? Can fraud be isolated or does it always spread like a cancer throughout the organization? Are the people who perpetuate the wrongdoing just *bad people*?

The answers to these questions are a mixed bag, and we'll address them throughout the book. But right now, let's answer these questions: What kind of frauds are we talking about? How common are they? Who are the actual perpetrators?

CHAPTER 2

Frauds of All Flavors

Most of us think of large companies or even gigantic publicly traded entities when we hear "corporate fraud," but the phrase could also describe fraud at any organization, regardless of size. "Corporate" comes from the Latin word, *corpus*, or body, and later the word, *corporare*, meaning, "form into a body." Just as a person's body is made up of many parts, so it goes with a business entity: its body parts are founders, executives, employees, customers, vendors, investors, and others.

I've been honored to speak at the national meetings of the Association of Certified Fraud Examiners (ACFE). They have a policy to not pay a conference speaker who is a former fraudster, but I'm happy to speak to their members anyway. In their 2014 *Global Fraud Study*, they focus on occupational fraud, which they define as "the use of one's occupation for personal enrichment through the deliberate misuse or misapplication of the employing organization's resources or assets."

I think this definition covers the entire spectrum of fraud in business today. The report certainly is a mix of large and small fraud cases. It contains an analysis of 1,483 cases of occupational fraud that occurred in more than 100 countries. Here's a summary:

- Forty-eight percent of them happened in the U.S.
- Most of them occurred either in privately owned businesses or publicly traded organizations.
- Small businesses (defined as those with fewer than 100 employees) were victimized in the greatest percentage of reported cases.

ETHICAL PLAY #2

"Complacency fosters unethical behavior."

Newton's first law of physics seems to apply to this: "An object either remains at rest or continues to move at a constant velocity, unless acted upon by an external force." People who commit large corporate frauds are in motion and hope those people observing the fraud will remain at rest.

But here's the part I find most interesting: the median losses for small businesses and the median losses for the largest entities (those with more than 10,000 employees) were almost identical, at $154,000 and $160,000, respectively. Of course, the impact of a $154,000 loss for most small businesses is much greater than the relative impact of a $160,000 loss at an organization with more than 10,000 employees!

The Frauds We Talk About Most

It's easy for us to examine larger corporate frauds for several reasons. For one thing, they seem to happen a lot. Plus, many of them involve the FBI, which means there's a good bit of information published about the frauds (although they are nearly three years behind on their posted website data). For instance, as of the end of 2011, various FBI field offices were pursuing 726 corporate fraud cases, several of which involved losses to public investors that individually exceed $1 billion. These cases resulted in 241 convictions, $2.4 billion in restitution orders, and $16.1 million in fines from corporate criminals.

From a jurisdiction standpoint, the scope of the FBI's fraud investigations is large and includes:

1. Falsification of financial information of public and private corporations, including:

- False accounting entries and/or misrepresentations of financial condition
- Fraudulent trades designed to inflate profit or hide losses
- Illicit transactions designed to evade regulatory oversight

2. Self-dealing by corporate insiders, including:

- Kickbacks
- Misuse of corporate property for personal gain
- Individual tax violations related to self-dealing

3. Insider trading—trading based on material, non-public information—including, but not limited to:

- Corporate insiders leaking proprietary information
- Attorneys involved in merger and acquisition negotiations leaking info
- Matchmaking firms facilitating information leaks
- Traders profiting or avoiding losses through trading
- Payoffs or bribes in exchange for leaked information

4. Obstruction of justice designed to conceal any of the above-noted types of criminal conduct, particularly when the obstruction impedes the inquiries of the SEC, other regulatory agencies, and/or law enforcement agencies.

So as you can imagine, with the exception of "mom and pop" incidents (like when a Minnesota woman who, during a seven-year period, siphoned off more than $230,000 from a church office where she worked), business frauds usually require a group of people to hide them, sustain them, and cover them up. Furthermore, these people—this *network* of fraudsters—can be identified.

CHAPTER 3

The Fraud Ecosystem

After years of thinking about my HealthSouth days and trying to understand what went wrong—with the company and with me—I have come to realize that the fraudulent activities may have only been executed by a handful of executives, but was supported by a number of others.

You've probably heard the saying, "It takes a village." That applies to corporate cheating, too. A miracle-cure website might pop up overnight as the result of one or two dishonest Internet entrepreneurs, but larger-scale frauds usually involve a sizable number of people with no intention of breaking the law or a professional code of ethics. They aren't like the real estate scammers exemplified in the Broadway play and 1992 film, *Glengarry Glen Ross*. That unsavory bunch knew they were acting unethically. In fact, deceit was key to the business model. While Jack Lemmon, Al Pacino, and the other phone salesmen may have started their business careers on the straight and narrow, they certainly understood what was expected of them when Alec Baldwin, who played a vile corporate "trainer" in the film, goaded them into a sales contest with a Cadillac El Dorado as first prize and a set of steak knives as second prize. "Third prize is you're fired," said Baldwin's character. "Get the picture?"

Getting the whole picture of a corporate fraud requires understanding the *ecosystem* in which cheating, fraud, and unethical behavior can flourish.

THE FRAUD ECOSYSTEM

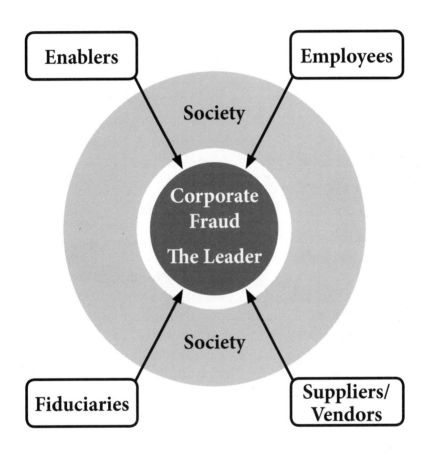

The size of the company really doesn't matter. The structure of the company doesn't matter either. Nonprofit organizations and churches can be ideal breeding grounds for fraud—in some cases better than a large, public company. Small companies, retail stores, e-commerce entities and mega-corporations—it's not about the size or structure of the organization, it's about the *people*. It's the people who make the trouble. People design the culture, decide the mission, determine how services will be sold, choose the vendors, and so on. And it's people who can decide whether to act ethically or not. I think you get the picture. To paraphrase a popular axiom, "Companies don't kill companies. People kill companies."

The Ecosystem Can Get Fouled

Huge corporate frauds are often attributed to a single individual. Examples include Bernard Madoff, Bernard Ebbers, and Dennis Koziowski. Over time we associate these people as the "fraudsters." However, these massive ethical breakdowns are complex. They happen in a business ecosystem that, allowing for scale and situation, looks very similar from case to case.

In our physical world, single polluters are not the only cause of environmental disasters. In the business ecosystem, cheating and unethical behavior are the pollutants, causing ultimate harm to everything and everyone they touch.

Think about it: the destruction of rainforests, the strip mining for coal, the spilling of oil, the dumping of pollutants into waterways—these are not the act of a single individual. Yes, maybe the captain of the *Exxon Valdez* oil tanker was sleeping off a bender when the giant ship hit a reef in Prince William Sound, Alaska, in 1989, spilling hundreds of thousands of barrels of oil and eventually covering 1,300 miles of coastline and 11,000 square miles of ocean. But others played a role in the mishap, like those who failed to repair iceberg-monitoring equipment onboard and the executives who made the financial decisions that led to an undersized and overworked crew. You might even make the case that—in an indirect way—Exxon's customers and stockholders were culpable.

Keeping the Lie Alive

A large-scale fraud may start with a CEO's intention of fixing the books to meet the company's projected quarterly earnings, but it never stops there. Keeping the lie alive requires a network of people to sustain it, support it, and conceal it. In this sense, the ecosystem of fraud is really a network of fraudsters. Who is in the network?

- The **leader** could be the founder, the CEO, the president, or all three.
- The **enablers** are usually key executives or close allies to the leader.
- **Employees** often know a fraud is being committed but are not at the center of it.
- **Fiduciaries** are typically not employees but have influence over the firm's ethical and financial behavior.
- **Vendors** (as illustrated in the Just for Feet example) can often participate in a fraud.
- **Society**, including customers, stockholders, and government entities, can also have a role.

How can so many good, hard-working people become involved in an organization's unethical behavior? Have we lost all sense of right and wrong? Has society devolved to the point that we no longer have our priorities straight? The 2014 edition of *Webster's Dictionary* defines success as "the fact of achieving of wealth, respect, or fame." Maybe we should go back the 1806 definition in Webster's: "being generous, prosperous, healthy, and kind."

ETHICAL PLAY #3

"Don't waive your conflict policy."

St. Augustine's quote certainly applies here: "Complete abstinence is easier than perfect moderation."

No contracting with friends, family, and other relatives is the best practice.

CHAPTER 4

The Leader

Marianne Jennings is an emeritus professor of legal and ethical studies at the W. P. Carey School of Business at Arizona State University. In her book, *The Seven Signs of Ethical Collapse: How to Spot Moral Meltdowns in Companies...Before It's Too Late*, Jennings discusses the bigger-than-life CEO who is often at the center of the fraud. She quotes Dennis Kozlowski, the former CEO at Tyco, who said, "I hire them just like me; smart, young, wants to be rich."

The community, media, and nearly everyone at a distance adore these iconic CEOs. However, the admiration from employees is often developed out of fear on several levels. They fear that challenging the legendary CEO may result in a stagnated career or outright firing. After all, these Super Leaders, as I call them, only want input from their employees if it agrees with what they already want. Over time, the management team around the Super Leader becomes sycophantic. They become yes-men and yes-women. To quote Jennings, they fail to realize that they play the role of useful idiots for the diabolical CEO.

Ken Lay, CEO of Enron, was able to impress stock analysts with his charm. The analysts did not want to challenge the legendary CEO because, after all, they might be wrong about the company. The media gave Lay a pass based on the financial glory he seemed to represent.

Bernie Ebbers was the iconic CEO of WorldCom. He was bigger than life and often quirky—all color, charm and command. He conveyed the same charisma whether he was home in Jackson, Mississippi, or on Wall Street. He surrounded

ETHICAL PLAY #4

"Curb your CEO."

Abraham Lincoln said, "Nearly all men can stand adversity, but if you want to test a man's character, give him power."

David Brin, an American scientist and award-winning author said, "It is said that power corrupts, but actually it's more true that power attracts the corruptible. The sane are usually attracted by other things than power."

The CEO of a public company is in a position of great power. It is the job of the board of directors and other fiduciaries to monitor and control that power. Marianne Jennings points out that often large corporate frauds start with an out-of-control CEO. The signs of his power abuse are usually very visible. If the board of directors does not take action, then they are part of the problem.

himself with a young management team he could control. His board of directors was nicknamed Bernie's Boys. Ebbers had sole discretion in setting salaries and bonuses to key employees. He made multimillionaires out of the company's officers.

Tyco's Dennis Kozlowski was named CEO of the year in 2001 by *Business Week* magazine. He came from very humble beginnings, which is a trait of many iconic CEOs. His desire to have more of everything—to the point of wretched excess—was fulfilled by doing whatever it took.

What Super Leaders Have in Common

Many of these Super Leaders have the same traits. They:

- Never like to be told they are wrong
- Never like to be told no
- Rarely own up to their mistakes
- Like to be the center of attention
- Want to win at all costs
- Are convinced that winning is measured by the accumulation of wealth
- Believe losing their wealth is a bigger deal than making more
- Are willing to squander the company's money to buy glory for themselves
- Are considered the darlings of Wall Street or their industry—at least for awhile.

The easiest of these traits to measure is their accumulation of wealth. Mr. Ebbers' net worth in 1999 was $1.4 billion, which put him number 174 among the richest Americans—and a very big fish in the small Mississippi pond. Among his possessions were ranches, hockey teams, a fly-fishing resort, a lumberyard, a plantation, and two farms with 20,000 head of Hereford cattle. The trappings of wealth were important to Mr. Kozlowski.

In 2001, he held the number-two spot for American CEO compensation at $411 million. His Fifth Avenue apartment cost $16.8 million plus $3 million to renovate and $11 million to furnish. Much of this expense was paid directly by Tyco.

Greed appears to be the primary motivating factor for these fraudsters. Sometimes it's not just the amount; it's the status it brings. Marianne Jennings reminded me of a very wealthy executive who, through information he gained from serving on multiple Fortune 100 boards, fed insider information to a large hedge fund. When asked why he did it, he said he wanted to be a member of the Billionaire's Club. "It's not that he wanted the money, he just wanted to be part of that exclusive New York crowd. He wanted to run in the big leagues."

Then again, some Super Leaders could be defined as nearly sociopathic. They do well in power professions like business and finance. This leader has one great advantage over others in these professions: no conscience. This frees him of many restraints others have. He is often enabled by his ability to superficially charm and seduce other people with his charisma.

We'll look at these extreme leaders more in Section 2. For now though, let's look at the next person in the fraud environment, the enabler.

CHAPTER 5

The Enabler

Enablers are the right and left hands of the leader. They have good business sense and understand right from wrong, but participate in the fraud for various reasons. They usually report directly to the leader. They typically do not initiate the fraud but play a key role in its perpetuation.

Enablers intrigue me the most because I was one of them, but I don't use this as an excuse for my criminal behavior. In fact, the Super Leader cannot pull off huge corporate frauds like HealthSouth without enablers. The failure of the CFO to do his or her job in an ethical manner is often at the heart of these frauds.

So what makes CFOs - the classic enablers - take part in these frauds? Often it's fear. Fear of losing the job. Fear of losing the boss's favor. Fear of losing the wealth or status they have attained. Enablers often lack the courage to face the difficult truth.

Dr. Dan Ariely sheds a lot of light on this question. He is a *New York Times* bestselling author and the James B. Duke Professor of Psychology and Behavioral Economics at Duke University with appointments at the Fuqua School of Business, the Center for Cognitive Neuroscience, Department of Economics, and the School of Medicine. He earned one PhD in cognitive psychology and another in business administration.

In March of 2012, I received a phone call from a film company representative who explained she was doing a documentary film on some of Dr. Ariely's work. (As of the close of 2014, the film, *(Dis)Honesty: The Truth About Lies*, is in post-production.) She invited me to New York City to film an interview with Dr. Ariely. I soon learned he was one of the most respected professors in his field and well known for his work in behavioral economics.

His 2012 book, *The (Honest) Truth About Dishonesty*, asks and answers these questions:

- Does the chance of getting caught affect how likely we are to cheat?
- How do companies pave the way for dishonesty?
- Does collaboration make us more honest or less so?
- Does religion improve our honesty?

His conclusions are backed by research and I found one study that was particularly relevant to my question, "What makes the enabler take part in frauds?"

Don't Show Me the Money

Dr. Ariely makes the case that people are more likely to commit dishonest acts when removed directly from cash. For example, you might take a box of paperclips from your office desk to use at home, but it is highly unlikely that you would take $3.50 from the petty cash box—even if you turned around and used the money to buy paperclips for home use. Dr. Ariely worries that the more cashless our society becomes, the more our moral compass will slip. I believe this played a role in my crime. Although I had the opportunity to steal from HealthSouth by writing any number of bogus checks, I didn't. Illegally changing accounting records to elevate the price of HealthSouth stock, however, didn't feel like thievery to me at the time. I knew it was wrong but I did not think of myself as a criminal.

We all know people who would be insulted if you were to suggest that they had stolen cash, but virtually all of them have taken part in some form of cheating that benefited them

ETHICAL PLAY #5

"Define issues by what's right and honest."

Accounting fraud often begins in the grey areas of accounting. Management may rationalize that an issue is grey and therefore there is no right answer. This is the wrong approach. The effort should be made to find the right answer and not the answer that helps the bottom line in the short run.

financially—like on their taxes, padding an insurance claim, or lying on a home loan application.

In Section 2, we'll look at more examples of Dr. Ariely's work and how it applies to ethical behavior.

Short-term Comfort

Understanding why enablers take part in frauds can also be explained by how we focus on short-term considerations at the expense of long-term concerns. Max H. Bazerman, the Jesse Isidor Straus Professor of Business Administration at Harvard Business School, talks about this in his book, *Blind Spots: Why We Fail to Do What's Right and What to Do About It* (co-authored with Ann E. Tenbrunsel).

Enablers let themselves believe that delivery of short-term results is more important than long-term results. A good example would be quarterly earnings reports. Missing Wall Street expectations today will almost certainly result in negative consequences tomorrow—like a reduced stock price, unhappy stockholders, and maybe lawsuits. The desire for comfort *now* is very powerful. For instance, would you prefer to receive $1,000 today or $1,180 a year from now? In controlled experiments, many people choose the former, despite having the opportunity to earn an 18% return. In years past, cities dumped their raw sewage into nearby rivers because it was a cheap and quick way for their citizens to rid their homes of waste. Little concern was given to the potential of long-term environmental damage. Here's what Dan Ariely has to say about that.

> Here's the thing. If you think about banking or politics, it's good for the bankers right now to get paid the way they get paid, but it's not good for the profession as a whole because nobody respects them and nobody trusts them. So by doing these things they are benefiting short-term but sacrificing the quality of their profession long-term. I

am hopeful that there will be some regulations and that some people will just start caring long-term and implement some broader changes in their organizations to take into account the long-term negative consequences of losing trust. You see, trust is a public good. If we all trust each other, life is really, really much, much better. If we stop trusting each other, then all kinds of things deteriorate and we pay a high price for it. It's something we really need to figure out and improve.

The growth of the national debt in the United States and many other countries is a result of the unintentional unethical behavior resulting from over-discounting the future. We have seen how unpopular it is to cut spending or increase taxes to reduce the debt. Why? Because that will take place now. You will feel the pain of it now. Delaying the pain until a future date dulls the pain—for now, anyway.

This may shed some light on how some enablers (and others in the ecosystem of fraud) rationalize bending the rules when faced with what Marianne Jennings calls the "decision point," which we'll examine in the next chapter.

CHAPTER 6

The Employee

The employees within companies experiencing fraud are part of the problem. It certainly is a problem if they are knowingly, actively taking part in the fraud. It is also a problem if they are aware of the fraud but do nothing to bring it to an end.

When I say employees, I mean those lower in rank than the leader and his key enablers. In smaller companies, these employees may not be part of the problem, but in the cases of the mega frauds we've discussed so far, these employees usually either take part or remain silent. Outside of the ringleaders (the leader and enablers), these are the people nearest the fire. They are inside the company observing all the details of the business. They know what is going on.

Why Do They Do It?

Employees participate in fraud for reasons that are different than upper level management. Huge financial gain is not one of the reasons. They probably do not see the big picture. Their supervisors lie to them as to why the rules are being broken and assure them that there is no problem. Often employees will see through these lies but they still do what their boss asks them to do. Why? Fear of losing their job is the primary reason. Loyalty to their boss may also play a big role in their helping with the fraud. Unfortunately, the supervisor will select employees he knows respect and like him. He will play on their emotions. I saw this firsthand at HealthSouth.

While the employee is motivated by fear and loyalty, he also will turn to rationalization to help him justify his behavior.

He will tell himself that it's not his job to worry. That what he is doing is not that important in the big picture. That it will not be an ongoing activity.

Many of these large corporate frauds take place at companies that appear to be huge success stories. The rank and file employees are proud to be a part of the company success. WorldCom, HealthSouth, and Enron were at one point considered the best Wall Street could offer. The top executives were considered the best in the country. It is somewhat understandable that the employees would want to help keep the dream alive. These companies are much like the super athlete that fans love to love. People will look the other way when these athletes break the rules, and the same is true for high-flying companies.

The outward appearance of a great financial success can encourage employees to stay silent and play along with the fraud. Although it may not be the main reason they participate, the windfall benefits they receive can be addictive. They may have purchased company stock or received a bonus because of the cooked books. The money associated with a fraud can corrode employees' sense of ethics while they still consider themselves good people. This belief can be reinforced if they see many other employees behaving the same way.

Even employees with no knowledge of the cheating can be affected. If the company's wrongdoing has been going on for years, the corrupt culture will degrade motivation and perpetuate lackluster work. These employees are discouraged from asking hard questions and the fraud keeps growing.

The Moment the Fraud Starts

In one of my conversations with Professor Marianne Jennings, she told me that, as a learning exercise, she walks her Arizona State University graduate-level accounting students through the "decision points" from various fraud case studies. In many of these real-life scenarios, no bags of money are exchanged

ETHICAL PLAY #6

"Always being ethical may not put you on the fast track."

A single decision can greatly alter the path we take and the strength of our integrity. Social scientists Tavris and Aronsen use the example of two college students who are struggling on an exam that will determine if they get into graduate school. They are "identical in terms of attitudes, abilities, and psychological health," and are "reasonably honest and have the same middling attitude towards cheating." Both students are presented with the chance to see another student's answers and both struggle with the temptation. But one decides to cheat and the other does not. "Each gains something important, but at a cost; one gives up integrity for a good grade, the other gives up a good grade to preserve his integrity."

and no arms are twisted. "I have to get my students at that point, that moment, when the fraud starts and get them to ask themselves what they could have done differently at the point where they could have changed the outcome," she says.

To accomplish this, she asks her students to think about a simple workplace scenario that might have quietly birthed the fraud. She recalls imagining with her students:

> Let's say these two guys used to work for the same auditing firm and now one of them is the chief accounting officer. They walk into the room and say, "How are the kids? How are things going?" It's a friendly conversation. They know each other. They trust each other. And one of them says, "You know this arrangement (whatever it might be) is temporary. It's just this one time if you can hang in with us." Or maybe it's, "Okay, the permit was denied but we'll appeal it and there's an election coming up and there's going to be a city council change."
>
> The students have to understand what those moments sound like, what their role would be, how they would perceive it. Because it's absolutely wrong. Nobody disagrees. But they do it anyway. So the focus has to be what the fraud looks like in its early stages. You're trying to have them imagine how the interpersonal aspect works when you have a relationship with this person. So in our classes we look at decision points and what they look like in the real world.

Before delving too far into casework with her accounting students, however, she tries to get them thinking more broadly about ethical behavior.

We start with non-accounting situations to look at the right and wrong, like a college football scandal. It gets them out of their accounting thinking. It allows them to identify with those in the middle of these situations and there's no risk for them to get it wrong because it's not accounting. Then they are able to recognize the common elements: it didn't happen overnight, there were decision points along the way, and at any point, they probably could have done something to prevent what eventually happened, which was a lot of harm to a lot of people. It's training them to understand that there really are some pretty bright lines out there, right and wrong. They've been taught for so long that there are no bright lines and that it's all grey.

Speaking of grey areas, that's all some fiduciaries see. We take a look at their ethical dilemmas next.

CHAPTER 7

The Fiduciary

Fiduciaries are typically not employees but have influence over the firm's ethical and financial behavior. Boards of directors, external auditors, regulatory agencies, stock analysts, and securities-rating agencies are examples. Fiduciaries have a huge responsibility to the public. If they don't perform their jobs properly, the public is at much greater risk of becoming victim of corporate fraud.

Conflicts Everywhere

There are many reasons why fiduciaries can do a poor job of serving the public. There is little doubt that the elephant in the room is conflict of interest. Board members, audit firms, investment bankers, rating agencies, and public officeholders are, in some way or another, compensated by the entity they should be monitoring. This is a very basic conflict of interest. Enron's auditor, Arthur Andersen, charged consulting and auditing fees totaling over $50 million.

To earn these fees, Andersen had a perpetual presence in the Enron's offices. Over time, the auditor's employees and Enron's employees became good friends. They traveled, lunched, and golfed together, and even celebrated each other's birthdays in the office. Many Enron employees were uncertain who worked for Andersen and who worked for Enron. Enron's accounting staff had many former Andersen employees. Seven former Andersen accountants became Enron employees in 2000 alone. There is little doubt that the close personal relationship between Andersen and Enron employees resulted in a willingness by Andersen to go along with unacceptable accounting procedures at Enron.

Boards Can Be a Problem

Virtually all of the large corporate frauds during the late 1990s and early 2000s involved companies with a weak board of directors. They were guilty of letting their CEO do as he pleased. In April 1999, Ken Lay, CEO of Enron, said he expected his handpicked board to "give a lot of really good advice, but not too much of it."

Compensation isn't the only conflict of interest. Many board members are good friends with management. The Tyco board was an assemblage of Kozlowski insiders. While the Enron board members had impressive pedigrees—a business school dean, several CEOs, an economist, a British accounting expert—it was still basically a good old boys club. All of them were very loyal to Ken Lay.

Fingerprints Everywhere

Investment bankers have fiduciary responsibility to many groups of people. Certainly they are responsible to their clients when assisting with public offerings and other capital-raising activities. They are asked to give "fairness opinions" concerning transactions before they take place. They also make recommendations to the customers that trade securities with them.

However, investment bankers, whether through official or unofficial dealings, have played a roll in the recent mega frauds and the subprime calamity. It always comes down to conflict of interest, and when conflicts concern huge, and I mean huge, sums of money there is great opportunity for complete ethical meltdowns. Dr. Ariely, in one of his YouTube videos, states that bankers are put in situations that almost guarantee they will fail ethically. The bankers for Enron were recommending the stock until almost the bitter end. The money was just too good.

The conflicts involving large sums of money in the banking industry are almost too long to list, but I would like to discuss one prominent position that faces conflict of interest at every turn: the Wall Street analyst.

Not Just a Cheerleader

While I was the CFO of HealthSouth, the analyst was probably the person from the investment banking firms I dealt with the most. I left HealthSouth in 1997. I have had no contact with any of the analysts since then except for one: Deborah J. Lawson. She began her career on Wall Street in 1988 and retired in 2005. I renewed my contact with her after her retirement. It has been a very gratifying experience. We are both "out of the game" and can talk openly about business issues in a manner we could not before. She read my first book and we have been speakers together at a couple of conferences.

After graduating from the University of Virginia with a finance degree in 1988, she began work on the 65th floor of Two World Trade Center for Dean Witter Reynolds. She was 22 years old. One of the first things she learned is that the investment banking side of the business is highly transaction-oriented. Once a deal is closed, the bankers are looking for the next deal. They stick with the companies if they think there

ETHICAL PLAY #7

"Have a strong board."

Obviously this is easier said than done. For certain, you want your board members to have the backbone, experience, and expertise to stand up to the iconic CEO and behave proactively in getting both performance and information from officers and employees.

are more deals to be done, but once a deal is done, they pretty much move on. The equity analyst (part of the equity research department) will continue to follow the company daily in an investment research role.

Deb moved on to a more prestigious firm, Alex Brown & Sons, where she started to really see and deal with the conflicts. She had trained herself to be a real researcher. She wasn't just a cheerleader for the companies, regurgitating what the companies told her, although a lot of analysts made, and continue to make, a fortune doing just that.

Managing the Conflicts

HealthSouth had been a very profitable client for Alex Brown long before Deb joined the firm. Over time, she became very close with several members of the HealthSouth management team, even going to some company parties in Birmingham. In fact, she attended my charity crawfish boil/music festival in Birmingham several times with about 5,000 other people.

From Alex Brown she moved up to Morgan Stanley & Co. At this point things started to change even more. She started to feel the pressure to be ranked highly each year in the *Institutional Investor* magazine poll. An analyst's ranking in this poll dramatically impacts compensation. Deb made it to the #2 spot for a few years.

During the late 1990s, Deb really had a difficult situation to maneuver. She correctly surmised through her research that some sectors of the healthcare industry were going to have a hard time due to Medicare reimbursements changes. She began to cool her enthusiasm toward some of the stocks she had been following. She quickly learned that some of her investing clients weren't happy when she made less than positive comments about stocks they owned. To her utter shock, when she made the slightest cautious comments about a stock or sector (not a downgrade, just some cautionary comments), she would often receive irate voice mails from investing clients saying she was not being "helpful."

So many conflicts to manage! She found herself spending hours trying to wordsmith reports about problems with a business or company. There was no way to please all the constituents that needed pleasing. The bankers wanted to do deals but no company would give their business to a firm that wasn't writing favorable research about it.

To put this into context, look at the money involved. Deb told me that a banker doing lots of deals could make $5 million or more annually. A slow year could be less than $1 million. This is very measurable pressure!

The conflicts of interest are built into the job of a research analyst. You develop relationships with a company's key executives, have dinners with them and fly around on road shows with them. You know when their children are born, when they get a new puppy, or when they are stressed because of operational issues. And, of course, you realize that your success rides on the success of their company and its stock price performance.

When you get to be an influential analyst on the Street, your comments and recommendations carry a certain weight. If you change a rating from buy to sell (which almost never happens, even today, but the same holds true for just a slight downgrade), you're not only creating waves in your own firm and with your investing clients but also for these people with whom you've actually developed a personal relationship. There are the rare company executives who won't hold a grudge or go ballistic, but she only ran into one or two of them.

Deb did an admirable job with all of these conflicts and finally landed at Goldman, Sachs & Co. and Citigroup before she quit the game in 2005 near the top of the mountain.

Apple Stands Up

The absurd importance Wall Street puts on companies to produce ever-increasing earnings can have a negative impact on
companies, resulting in unethical or even fraudulent behavior
on the part of management. But there are examples of leaders
doing and saying the right thing, regardless of the fallout.

Take Apple, for instance. In 2013, Apple stock hit $103 but
by mid-year it was at $68—down by 34% during this period,
when it seemed to me every fourth person on the planet owned
an Apple iPhone. But the Street was not happy. I guess they
wanted every *other* person on the planet to own an iPhone.

Tim Cook, CEO of Apple (and an Alabama native), was
asked at the March shareholders meeting about the return on
investment (ROI) from Apple's commitment to making facto-
ries carbon-neutral and removing harmful chemicals from its
products. Cook showed an uncharacteristic flash of real anger.
"I don't consider the bloody ROI," he said. "If you want me to do
things only for ROI reasons, you should get out of this stock."
The crowd erupted into raucous applause. I, too, applaud his
stance. CEOs need to constantly tell the Street it is not always
about short-term earnings.

Managing the Business, Not the Numbers

My father was a sole proprietor. In my mind, he was very successful. He put all five of his children through college, and we
all earned degrees. He never had to report quarterly earnings
to investors and worry that his financial net worth would go
down or that he would be fired because he missed his numbers.
He had up and down years, but he just adjusted his personal
spending when business was down. Many times the business
was down because of the overall economy, not because he was
doing a poor job running his business. My father was a very
happy person and I believe a very ethical businessman. He

truly managed his business, not his numbers.

Yes, the times are different now. But somehow we have moved away from the fundamentals of business management to an obsession for instant results. We need to remember that, sometimes, it's about doing what's best for long-term earnings growth and preservation. Sometimes it's just about doing the right thing and letting the chips fall where they may.

CHAPTER 8

The Vendor

Just for Feet is a good example of how vendors and suppliers can collaborate in a fraud. In this case, a customer (Just for Feet) who seemed too important to anger or lose altogether pushed the shoe manufacturers and suppliers into committing fraud.

You Scratch My Back

There's an old saying in certain sales cultures: "Nothing happens until somebody sells something." In many ways, that is true. The process of selling something, acquiring new customers, and maintaining existing ones is essential to business success. To achieve those objectives, the seller often becomes chummy with the buyer. It's human nature to do favors for someone who is in a position to help you. There's nothing wrong with it. Unless it stretches into unethical behavior.

It is also human nature to want to return favors. We want to be good to those who treat us well. Dr. Ariely has done research in the area of the hidden cost of favors. His experiments suggest that once someone (or some organization) does us a favor we became partial to anything related to the giving party—and that the magnitude of this bias increases as the magnitude of the initial favor increases.

The 14,000 registered lobbyists in Washington represent a type of vendor. The product they are selling is point of view. They spend a small fraction of their time informing politicians about actual facts and a large part of their time trying to implant a feeling of obligation in the politicians. They hope sowing seeds of "goodwill" with the politicians and policy makers

ETHICAL PLAY #8

"Being ethical means you have to speak up."

The English philosopher Edmund Burke said, "The only thing necessary for the triumph of evil is for good men to do nothing."

A number of good companies are starting whistleblower programs that make it less difficult for good men—and women—to speak up when they see wrongdoing in the organization.

will ensure that they reap a harvest of favor.

Dr. Ariely's viewpoint on this matter, as he told me in 2014, is pretty clear.

> A lot of things are wrong in D.C. I think the first one is lobbying. Lobbying is a type of profession that is designed to create conflicts of interest in politicians. They're very, very successful and they do it in all kinds of ways, right? It's really nice that buying somebody a sandwich and a beer gets them to see life from your perspective. As people, it is wonderful because you can meet people, you can buy them coffee, and they like you a little bit more and start seeing life from your perspective. Once you do it in lobbying, that's incredibly dangerous because now it means that you could buy somebody and for even small amounts of money they can see life from your perspective. One thing we need to do is eliminate or at least highly constrain lobbying.
>
> I think we need to eradicate some standards that are so flexible that it's hard to know what they really are. But I am optimistic that we can do it. It's not going to be easy. It's going to take a long time, it will require people to understand what is going on, and they will have to have the will to do it.

Pharmaceutical companies typically have reps whose job is to visit doctors and convince them to purchase medical equipment or prescribe drugs from their firm. Gifts are given. They may be small, such as pens and mugs, but in previous years, doctors often received tickets to sporting events and paid vacations.

Vendor Fraud in a Nutshell

Vendor fraud can be divided into two groups: fraud committed by vendors acting alone and fraud involving collusion between vendors and the defrauded organization's employees.

An example of a hybrid of those two groups is a common occurrence: a supplier submits unwarranted invoices over a period of years—sometimes operating with the help of an insider who is accepting kickbacks.

Common vendor fraud schemes include:

- **Overbilling.** Vendors submit inflated invoices for their goods and services.
- **Bid rigging.** Vendors and employees conspire to steer a company's purchase of goods or services to a particular bidder.
- **Price fixing.** This is an agreement between competing vendors to set the same price or price range for goods or services.
- **Kickbacks.** Here, employees accept misappropriated funds from vendors for facilitating fraud.

Next, we'll take a look at one more part of the fraud network. Could members of our society—you and me—be partly to blame?

CHAPTER 9

Society

To some degree, society influences the level of ethical behavior in the business world. When people are complacent about unethical practices around them, they are part of the problem.

Early in U.S. history, slavery was legal and even accepted, especially in the South, as a business practice. People accepted it as an economic necessity. Today we would certainly consider owning another human as an unethical practice.

Then the Industrial Revolution swept the nation—and introduced the era of the robber barons. The barons were businessmen who used what we would consider now to be exploitative practices to amass their wealth. These men paid extremely low wages, provided atrocious working conditions, and squashed competition by acquiring competitors in order to create monopolies. The barons had great influence at high levels of the government. Included in the list are John Astor, Andrew Carnegie, Henry Flagler, Andrew Mellon, J. P. Morgan, John Rockefeller, and Leland Stanford.

Society benefited from these unethical practices in many ways. Many would say the robber barons helped build the modern foundation for our country's role as a world superpower.

Then and Now

Society—meaning individuals like you and me—also benefited from the stock market bubble created by unethical business practices in mortgage and banking that led to the 2008 economic meltdown. Many people built big houses with borrowed money they knew they would have trouble repaying. Some took

ETHICAL PLAY #9

**"Just because it's legal doesn't
mean it's ethical."**

advantage of "zero down" new automobile loans that seemed too good to be true.

In his book, *Wall Street Values*, Dr. Michael A. Santoro writes that, "The financial crisis was fundamentally a crisis of business ethics rooted in almost three decades of moral, financial, and institutional transformation on Wall Street."

If society was partially to blame for that mess, we certainly paid dearly. By one Federal Reserve estimate, the country lost almost an entire year's worth of economic activity—nearly $14 trillion—during the recession from 2007 to 2009. The deep and persistent losses of the recession forced states to make broad cuts in spending and public workforces. For businesses, the recession led to changes in expansion plans and worker compensation. And for individual Americans, it has meant a future postponed. The burst of the housing bubble devastated the real estate market, leaving millions facing foreclosure, millions more underwater, and generally stripping Americans of years' worth of accumulated wealth.

Still a Long Way to Go

The good news is that, I believe, we are improving our ethical behavior in society as time passes. Volunteerism among young people has increased dramatically over the years. Concern for the environment, once the domain of a relatively few activists, is mainstream. Social media allows us to know in seconds when wrong has been done. Behavior is becoming more and more transparent.

We've got a long way to go as a society, but after all, society is just a lot of individuals living and working together. In Section 3, we'll discuss ways to build *individual* ethical muscle. But first, let's examine why we humans have problems with personal integrity in the first place.

PART TWO: WHY WE CAN'T SEEM TO PLAY BY THE RULES

CHAPTER 10

The Liars and Cheats in Our Mirrors

In 1987, shortly after HealthSouth went public, an analyst from a small investment banking firm interviewed me. Little did I know that I would nearly lose my job because of it.

Up to this point, only our CEO had given interviews of this nature, but he and the analyst couldn't coordinate schedules. This was a big deal because I knew the analyst would write a research paper on HealthSouth and make one of three recommendations: a strong buy, buy and hold, or sell. She flew to our corporate offices in Birmingham and the interview lasted a couple of hours. Standard subjects for such an interview are company business model, marketing strategy, and size and types of markets and competition. The interviewer will also ask for a discussion on recent reported financial results and will try to get you to give a financial prediction for the next few years. Mostly for legal reasons you stay away from giving a firm forecast, but if the analyst throws out a number you can say if it's in the right ballpark or not. What you really want is for the analyst to say in her own words, "My financial forecast for the company is x." And then you hope that "x" is really good!

I felt the interview went well and that she was leaving with a good opinion of the company. Toward the end of the interview she asked me what could go wrong, since I had spent the last two hours talking about how great things were—something Wall Street calls "putting lipstick on the pig." I said I didn't think anything could go wrong. Then she said, "There must be something that occasionally keeps you awake at night."

I said no. (Remember, this was years before committing my first act of accounting fraud, which *would* keep me up at night.) She would not cease this line of questioning.

Finally, in a moment of candor, I said that investors and other people sometimes question what will happen if Medicare changes the way it reimburses the company for services. I told her this was not really a concern because there was a huge demand for our services from the private-pay sector and, in fact, we only marketed to the non-government payers—which was a higher-margin business. If we *were* to see a decrease in government money, I went on, it could easily be replaced with more profitable payers. She seemed to accept what I was saying.

About two weeks later, our stock price opened several dollars below the previous closing. The analyst had released her research paper with a "sell" recommendation accompanied by the comment, "HealthSouth CFO concerned about Medicare reimbursement." A very unpleasant meeting with the CEO followed. I told him the analyst had misrepresented what I had said. Later in the day, the CEO told me he had spoken to all of the board members by phone about why the stock had dropped so much—and that he had to convince some of the board members that I should not be fired. From that day forward I was much less honest and open with the investment community.

Learning to Lie

Today, I don't regret having been honest in that interview, but what I do regret is how, as the CFO of a New York Stock Exchange company, I allowed that incident to change my attitude and had a negative effect on the way I reported the financial results of the company.

Sure, before then I had told lies, but it wasn't part of my general makeup. I considered myself an honest person. But after that day, I learned that if I wanted to stay on the exciting rollercoaster called HealthSouth, I would have to learn to lie—and to do it well.

All humans have the capacity to be dishonest and are, in fact, dishonest in varying degrees a good bit of the time. Research proves it. To some extent, our reality—the way we interact with others and see the world in general—is shaped by our motivations. When being honest gets us what we want, great. But sometimes we tend to want that thing so badly that we are willing to trade our honesty for it. That thing could be money, status, sex, acceptance, fame, power—the list goes on.

This is why top management can be very conflicted when reporting to investors. The CEO and CFO, rightly or not, are generally considered to be doing a good job when the company stock is increasing in value. Their wealth and job security depends on an up-ticking stock. Just as football coaches use "coach speak" (saying a lot but not communicating much) and politicians try to communicate in media sound bites, top business executives have to speak in a code that straddles the line between what investors want to hear and the SEC demands to know. Living in this conflicted world was part of being a CFO that I disliked very much. I trained myself to lie.

From then on, the lies that I told on behalf of HealthSouth, both small and large, were all decision points that ultimately led me to committing fraud and being sent to prison for it. The problem with learning to lie is that lying becomes your go-to tactic when things get tough. It's easy to learn to lie; it's not so easy to unlearn it.

Boiling the Frog

The most often asked question after I have given a speech about the fraud at HealthSouth is, "When did you cross the line?" That's actually tougher to answer than you might think.

There were many decision points. There were days when I didn't speak up when someone else in the company lied. There were other signs and indicators that I should have recognized as dangerous, but either ignored them or rationalized them.

Certainly in the rearview mirror I can see plenty more than I did at the time. But when you're in it, you usually don't "cross the line" all of a sudden. There may not be a distinct line that you cross. Often it's gradual. It starts small and grows larger over time, until you have trouble recognizing the line.

I've heard that if you put a frog in boiling water he'll hop out. But if you put him in cool water, a comfortable environment for a frog, and gradually increase the heat to boiling, he won't try to react until it's too late.

At HealthSouth, we dipped our pasty legs into the cool water of "interpretive accounting" long before we started making false entries in the official accounting ledgers. One example was creative statistical reporting. In most businesses with multiple operating units investors want to know about your same store volume growth. They value growth from existing units more than growth from the creation or acquisition of new units. As the rate of growth in our old stores began to decline, we started reporting larger cities as one store.

For example, as we would open a second location —in a large city such as Dallas, Miami, Atlanta or Chicago—we would report all volume coming from the first store. After all, we reasoned, in many cases the new store was run by the manager of the first store and the second store did not have its own business office yet. Of course, we never disclosed all of this to the investing public. Over time, the store statistics were just made up in order to keep them looking good. Were we breaking the law? It was not part of our actual financial records. It was certainly unethical behavior. We were being deceptive. We were lying.

The Fudge Factor

In *The (Honest) Truth About Dishonesty*, Dan Ariely tells about experiments that led to his "fudge factor theory," which is central to much of his book. Two groups of students were given five minutes to complete some arithmetic problems. In the first group, students were promised money for problems they completed correctly. They would finish the test and turn their answers in to the experimenter's desk. The paper was then graded on the spot and the students were paid for their correct answers. On average, students got four correct.

The second group of students, who were given the opportunity to cheat, was called the shredder group. At the end of the five minutes the students were told the answers. They graded their own papers. They were told to put their worksheet through the shredder in the back of the room and then report to the experimenter how many correct answers they had. In other words, they were on the honor system.

The question was: would the shredder students cheat? And if so, by how much? To make this determination, Dan did a bit of deception of his own. The shredding machine the students *thought* was destroying the evidence was actually just shredding the edges of the paper but *sounded* like it was devouring the whole page!

Ariely and his colleagues found that, given the opportunity, many people did fudge their score. In the first group, participants solved an average of four out of twenty problems. But participants in the shredder group claimed to have solved an average of six—two more than the first group. And this overall increase did not result from a few individuals who claimed to solve a lot more problems, but from lots of people who cheated by just a little bit.

ETHICAL PLAY #10

"Make decisions putting your values first."

Most people have the right values but often fail to make them part of their decision making process. We know right from wrong; what we need is training on how to behave ethically.

Interestingly, when the amount of the reward was increased you would think the amount of cheating increased, but it actually went down slightly. Dr. Ariely believes these experiments show that, "our sense of our own morality is connected to the amount of cheating we feel comfortable with. Essentially we cheat up to the level that allows us to retain our self-image as a reasonably honest individual."

Hence, the fudge factor.

Dr. Ariely's book contends that our behavior is driven by two opposing motivations. On one hand, we want to view ourselves as honest people. On the other hand, we also want to benefit from cheating. Clearly these two motivations are in conflict. But how can we have both? This balancing act is the process of rationalizing. How much we can cheat before it starts feeling "sinful?"

I believe in the fudge factor theory. When I was the CFO at HealthSouth, I used to rationalize much of my unethical behavior. This was well before I took part in clearly illegal activities. I would justify bending the accounting rules by rationalizing that everyone was doing it and that it was the best option because many people would benefit and almost no one would get hurt. It seemed we were cheating just a little for the greater benefits it would bring. At the time I did not fully understand the mental game I was playing.

Is Cheating Cultural?

Dr. Ariely's research also suggests that cheating varies little between groups of people, even when looking at different nationalities. However, when you layer culture on top of these different groups, cheating does vary. The reason is that our culture helps us rationalize our level of cheating.

The recent financial crisis in Greece was exacerbated by

the attitude of some Greeks that not paying your taxes is acceptable behavior. The people of Greece were not born with a higher propensity to cheat on their taxes, but over time, it became the norm. As in Dr. Ariely's simple math test—many people cheating a little adding up to big money—millions of Greeks not paying their fair share of taxes contributed to the Greek economy becoming the weakest in Europe. An article in *The New Yorker* explains that Greek citizens have what social scientists call very low "tax morale." In most developed countries, most people pay their taxes in part because they feel a responsibility to contribute to the common good. Countries have high tax compliance when people feel they have some say in how the government acts. This may be why Americans, despite being anti-tax in their rhetoric, are fairly compliant taxpayers.

Many Greeks, by contrast, see fraud and corruption as ubiquitous in business and in the tax system. The result has been a vicious circle: because tax evasion is so common, people trust the system less, which makes them less willing to pay taxes. Because so many don't pay in, the government has had to raise taxes on those who do. This has resulted in protests and open riots. The new Greek government is trying hard to change things, but a social inclination toward tax evasion is hard to eradicate.

How We Act and How We Think We'll Act

In the book, *Blind Spots*, Dr. Max Bazerman explains that people can inherently believe their own ethicality despite the evidence to the contrary. Given a hypothetical ethical dilemma, people say they will make an ethical choice. But when actually faced with an ethical dilemma, they make an unethical choice.

He gives an example.

> Imagine that a young female college student is seeking on-campus employment to supplement her living expenses. She sees a help-wanted ad posted on campus for a research assistant. The hours and pay are just what she's looking for, so she immediately applies for the position. She is called in for an interview and meets with a man who appears to be in his early thirties. During the course of the interview, he asks her a number of standard interview questions, as well as the following three questions:
>
> - Do you have a boyfriend?
> - Do people find you desirable?
> - Do you think it is appropriate for women to wear bras to work?
>
> What do you think the young woman would do in this situation? If you think she would feel outraged and confront the interviewer about his inappropriate questions, you are not alone. A research study examined this exact situation. When asked to predict how they would behave in such an interview, 62% of female college students said they would ask the interviewer why he was asking these questions or tell him that the questions were inappropriate, and 68% said they would refuse to answer the questions.

These students' predictions may be unsurprising, yet they aren't accurate. In the same study, the researchers put female college students in the actual interview situation described above. A 32-year-old male interviewer actually asked them the offensive questions. What happened? None of the students refused to answer the questions. A minority of them asked the interviewer why the questions had been asked, but they did so politely and usually at the end of the interview.

There are endless examples of the human tendency to make inaccurate predictions about our own behavior. We believe we will behave a certain way in a given situation but, when actually faced with the situation, we do not behave as we thought we would. This might explain why we keep making New Year's resolutions that we don't keep. (In fact, am I alone or do you ever, in the back of your mind, *know* you will not keep that resolution, even as you are making it? That's a weird pairing of self-honesty and self-delusion.)

Do we really not know ourselves very well? Or are we willing to lie to ourselves to the extent that we are "comfortably numb" (as the rock song goes) in an ideal world of our own making? Or do we just blame our character flaws?

Other People Behaving Badly

A twist on Bazerman's research about predicting our own good behavior but acting differently is something social scientist Lee Ross called the "fundamental attribution error." This is the tendency to think that *other* people behave badly because they are bad people whereas *we* make mistakes because of a difficult situation.

This reminds me of something Marianne Jennings told me about one of her classes and the "little white lie."

"I did a survey with them," she said, "and 87% admitted that, in the past, they had complimented someone on their looks when they didn't mean it. Then I asked them, 'Have you ever put your name on a project when you didn't carry your share of the work?' Seventy-five percent of them said no, 25% said yes. Then I anonymously asked them, 'Have you ever seen anybody put their name on a project when they didn't do the work?' About

75% said yes, 25% said no. It was an absolute mirror flip! It was funny. Even the students laughed about that one."

Maybe We're All Just Hot Messes

So we think we are honest, but we're not. Then we find ways to get what we want by lying and cheating in small amounts—but only to the extent that we can still feel good about our fundamental honesty. We say we'll do one thing in a particular circumstance—the right thing—but we do something else. While we guard our own sense of personal integrity, we doubt the same in others.

Is it any surprise that, with all these internal conflicts raging, we often find ourselves in an ethical hot mess?

Unfortunately, that's only part of the larger business ethics picture. Our *circumstances* and the *external pressures* that accompany them have a powerful influence on how we act.

CHAPTER 11

Why Is It Hard to Do the Right Thing?

Making the choice to do the right thing is difficult. Even well-intentioned people can stumble into ethical minefields if they do not keep their antennae up and guard against errors in judgment that people are often predisposed to make.

When values are on the line, the process of choosing a course of action is often obscured by conflicts of interest—some of which we may not even be aware. Our well-developed ability to rationalize kicks in and makes the easy way out the easy choice to make.

An example is what the Institute for Global Ethics has labeled *truth versus loyalty.* This ethical dilemma involves someone who tries to trick us into rationalizing unethical behavior. A good example is when a sales manager tries to convince a salesman to use deceptive sales tactics to achieve the company sales goals. He is pitting truth against loyalty.

In the workplace, there are many common arguments or rationalizations that can muddle our brain when we try to take the ethical course of action:

- "Everyone does this, so it's standard practice. It's even expected."
- "The impact of this action is minimal. It does not really hurt anyone."
- "This is not my responsibility. I'm just following orders."
- "I know this isn't quite fair to the customer but I don't want to hurt my boss or my company."

As we begin to recognize the mental and verbal skirmishes we experience as we strive to become more ethical people, we will become more adept at finding and deploying responses to address them.

The Dark Forces of Unethical Decision Making

Robert Prentice outlines several biases in how people see a situation in which an ethical decision is required—and how they tend to behave. Maybe my reference to "dark forces" in this section is overdramatic since these biases are accepted social science and, therefore, neither good nor bad. But for our purposes, they do represent formidable challenges to ethical decision making in the business world and beyond.

Obedience to Authority. Studies have shown that people tend to be far more deferential to authority than they realize. Pleasing authority usually leads to rewards. Displeasing authority can get us fired. The research tells us that unethical actions happen more often when a person is urged by a superior than when he is acting on his own initiative.

Conformity Bias. People conform their behavior to those around them to avoid embarrassing workplace faux pas or a breach of office etiquette. How can this lead you to unethical decisions? Criticizing a colleague's behavior is difficult, and even more so when made on ethical grounds. Nobody wants to make an enemy of a co-worker; she might be your boss one day. Like Professor Dumbledore said in Harry Potter, "It takes a great deal of bravery to stand up to our enemies, but just as much to stand up to our friends."

Incrementalism. This is the slowly boiling frog, the slippery slope. Prentice notes that people often slide down a slippery slope in tandem with their peers in an organization (conformity). The bottom line is that people, over time, will adapt to a corporate culture that encourages and/or rewards

ETHICAL PLAY #11

"Trust your instincts."

As you accumulate knowledge—whether it's about what books your spouse likes or how to play chess—you begin to recognize patterns. Your brain unconsciously organizes these patterns into blocks of information—a process the late social scientist, Herbert Simon, PhD, called chunking. Over time, your brain chunks and links more and more patterns, then stores these clusters of knowledge in your long-term memory. When you see a tiny detail of a familiar design, you instantly recognize the larger composition—and that's what we regard as a flash of intuition. This elaborate brain circuitry likely evolved so our forebears could size up a person or a situation quickly.

So listen to your gut feelings instead of brushing them aside. Your intuition may not always steer you right, but it can be a useful first step in decision-making.

aggressive actions that push the envelope toward the unethical. Before they realize what's happening, they are acting in ways they don't like and never would have predicted.

Groupthink. Research psychologist Irving Janis coined this term for a very common occurrence in American business: when independent thinking is trumped by pressures from superiors and peers in a cohesive group, like a board, committee or department. In their effort to avoid introducing stress into their seeming solidarity, the group suppresses dissent and characterizes potential critics as "just not getting it."

Overoptimism. Many people, particularly leaders, can be so optimistic that they make bad decisions. It's probably safe to say that during the dot-com boom some stock analysts were overoptimistic about the prospects of the companies they were following—and sometimes investors who listened to them paid dearly.

Overconfidence. A lot of us are pretty sure we're better than the other guy, something Prentice calls an "irrational confidence in the accuracy of (a person's) decisions."

Self-Serving Bias. Most of us not only gather information in a self-serving way but also process it in a self-serving way. Even those who are trained to be objective and skeptical, such as auditors, tend to accept evidence that confirms their bias, while carefully scrutinizing evidence that's contrary to it. For instance, in the 1960s, after revelations about the harmfulness of smoking, tobacco manufacturers had a great deal of difficulty processing new information about the products' carcinogenic effects, thus creating ethical minefields.

Framing. Framing a question in two different ways can create two different responses. If you are facing a serious surgery, do you want the doctor to tell you about the 90% success rate or the 10% death rate? In business, when you focus only on one relevant aspect of an issue and minimize the others, you tend to see solutions only from that framing. For example, during my HealthSouth days, we were fixated on share price, which caused us to put most of our focus on Wall Street earnings projections. You know how that worked out!

Costs. Studies show that people will attend a play they have decided they really do not want to see simply because they have already spent money on the tickets. Pouring money into a sinking business despite all signs of failure is another example. What are the causes? Overconfidence and overoptimism are two. We've all thrown good money after bad, but at some point we have to save ourselves from trying to save the wrong things—and avoid behaving unethically in the process.

Loss Aversion. Studies show that people enjoy gains only about half as much as they suffer from losses. Loss aversion is related to the *endowment effect*, the idea that when we become attached to a thing, it becomes part of our *endowment* and therefore much more valuable to us than before we became attached to it. So, because it's so *ours* (think about the money in your 401k and what you would do if someone threatened to take it away) we might make unethical decisions to protect it—exerting far more energy than we expended to accumulate it in the first place.

The easiest example of this at HealthSouth is that, early on, we were in the building mode—literally and financially. A dozen years later, we had built up a sizable *endowment*: solid share growth, street cred in the healthcare industry, hundreds of locations and, personally, lots of money. All of this needed protecting. So when earnings started going south, even though we had no intention of behaving unethically, we made the decision to start committing fraud to protect that endowment.

Are these dark forces of unethical decision-making lurking in your workplace? I'm pretty sure they prowl every human mind and exist, at some level, in every organization. Knowing about them, and the ethical frailty they might expose, is the first step in defeating them.

CHAPTER 12

Emotions and Fraud

External pressures are noticeable and measurable once you know what to look for, but what isn't as obvious is the emotional element in committing fraud.

I just finished reading *A.B.C.'s of Behavioral Forensics*, which really drives home the point that, in just about everything we do, we are driven by emotions: enjoyment, interest, surprise, anger, fear, distress, disgust, contempt, and shame are just a few. Why should committing fraud be any different?

The authors' primary focus in the book is that fraud deterrence and detection should focus on how to deal with the underlying psychology of those in the fraud network. For my purposes, the most interesting reading was about the emotional makeup of those fraudsters like me and other enablers who "fall prey" to powerful Super Leaders who usually initiate the fraud.

Fruit Vendors and Fake Watches

Fraud requires the establishment of intent to deceive another. Desires such as greed, status, revenge, excitement, and parity are the key motives for fraud. Fraud is theft, but not by force. The authors say, "There is perhaps no aspect of fraud more important than this. There is no robbery at gunpoint. No direct threat of harm to the victim. Rather, the victim willingly gives away money or something of value. Fraud is a deception."

Deceiving people is part of human behavior. People use cosmetics to enhance their appearance—to color their lips, skin, or hair—and wear perfume to smell better. Misleading

ETHICAL PLAY #12

"The ethical finish first, eventually, and with peace of mind."

Telling the truth will rarely shame you, but lying can do you in forever. If you lie and succeed, you are deprived of feelings of accomplishment. Not only does the "achievement" do nothing to enhance your self-esteem, it actually undermines it since you must carry the burden of depriving others a fair shot at success.

George Bernard Shaw said, "The liar's punishment is not in the least that he is not believed, but that he cannot believe anyone else."

others by creating a false impression is called "apple polishing" for a fruit vendor and "window dressing" when used in financial statements. The question then becomes one of magnitude. This follows Dr. Ariely's fudge factor concept. He points out that people who wear fake designer watches may be inclined to cheat more in other areas, too.

Before I began to read the *A.B.C.* book, I had heard I was mentioned in it prominently. I believe the authors chose me and my relationship with Richard Scrushy as a good example of how emotions play a huge part in understanding fraud.

The authors make the case that the HealthSouth fraud episode was intriguing because it clearly outlines the method by which the bad apple (Richard) recruits willing accomplices to execute the fraud.

I Understand Better Now

I now see how these innate emotions led me down the path to commit fraud. In the beginning, I received great enjoyment from being a part of such a successful company and becoming wealthy. However, the pressure to continue meeting or beating Wall Street expectations was soon very stressful for me. Richard Scrushy kept turning up the pressure to hit the numbers. I should have challenged Richard about how he was presenting the company to the Street incorrectly. But I had learned from working with him that he didn't like to be told he couldn't do something. I began doing things out of fear—fear of Richard, fear of disappointing investors, and fear of not maintaining my wealthy lifestyle. I had become seduced by a cycle of excitement, enjoyment, fear, distress, and shame.

This paraphrased story from the *New Yorker* by singer and poet Patti Smith, which the authors use in their *A.B.C.'s* book, will help me make a point.

When she was ten years old, Patti lived with her family in a small ranch house in rural New Jersey.

Her family had little money. One day at the grocery store, a promotional display for the *World Book Encyclopedia* caught Patti's eye. The first volume was ninety-nine cents with a ten-dollar purchase.

As she walked with her mother looking for discounted food, the book was all she could think about. Finally, holding her breath as her mother counted out the crumpled bills from her wallet, Patti found the courage to ask for the encyclopedia. "It's only 99 cents," she pled.

"Not now, Patricia," her mother said sternly. "Today is not a good day." The little girl was crestfallen.

The next Saturday, her mother gave her a dollar and sent her to the store for milk and bread. Patti went straight to the World Book display. There was only one first volume left, which she placed in her cart. She didn't need a cart, but took one so she could read as she went up and down the aisles. After awhile, when she realized it was time to leave, she couldn't bear to part with the book. Impulsively, she put it inside her shirt and zipped up her windbreaker.

She went through the checkout, paid her dollar for the groceries and headed home with her heart pounding.

Then she felt a heavy tap on her shoulder and turned to find the biggest man she had ever seen. He was the store detective, and he asked her to hand it over. She nervously complied. He asked her why she stole the book and she admitted that she knew it was wrong. The man told her he would have to walk her home to tell her parents, but Patti promised to tell them as soon as she arrived. He agreed.

Her mother was agitated when she got home. "Where were you? I needed the bread for your father's sandwiches. I told you to come right home."

And suddenly, Patti's ears started ringing, She felt dizzy, and threw up.

Her mother tended to her immediately.

"What is it, Patricia? Did something bad happen?"

"Yes," she whispered. "I stole something."

She told her mother about her lust for the book, her wrongdoing, and the big detective. Her mother was a loving person but could be explosive, and the little girl tensed, waiting for the barrage of verbal punishment, the sentencing that always seemed to outweigh the crime. But she said nothing. She told Patti that she would call the store and tell the detective she had confessed. Then she urged Patti to sleep.

When Patti awoke, sometime later, the house was silent. Her mother had taken her siblings to the field to play. She sat up and noticed a brown-paper bag with her name on it. She opened it and inside was the *World Book Encyclopedia*, Volume I.

Emotions and Misdeeds

I relate to that story because of the shame the little girl felt when she acted contrary to her values. Shame was just one of the emotions that was involved in my criminal misdeeds. I was not only embarrassed at being betrayed by Richard, but sad at betraying myself, and, as the *A.B.C.* authors stated, "[ignoring] Scrushy's conceited and egomaniacal traits at [my] own peril."

Emotions were just one of the factors that compromised my role as a financial watchdog at HealthSouth. The tension between maintaining accounting professionalism and dealing with the constant pressure to produce good numbers created lots of grey areas that were formidable. Hopefully the next chapter will shine some light on these shadowy hazards for you.

CHAPTER 13

Shades of Grey

One of my friends from Wall Street days is Bruce Cozadd. Bruce co-founded Jazz Pharmaceuticals, a successful public company that now has over 800 employees across multiple countries. Bruce, who serves as the company's chairman and CEO, started a quarterly speaker series to highlight the company's values and invited me to Palo Alto to be the first speaker in the series.

Jazz is different. The company does a lot of good for the patients who depend on the medicines it makes, but it also has a strong ethical core that seems authentic and comes from the top down.

Recently, Bruce introduced me to one of his key people, Eric Fink, the global head of learning and development and employee communications. Eric says that Jazz manages some of the inherent risks in his industry by making sure that decisions aren't made in silos. Here's what he told me.

> I think there are a lot of grey areas in our business. There are complex laws and regulations around promotion, how we interact with healthcare professionals, how we interact with patients, and how we conduct our clinical trials.
>
> One way we manage that complexity links back to one of our values, collaboration: When one of us encounters a grey area, rather than making a call in isolation, we pull together a diverse set of people to make the right decision as a team. That practice stems from the reason that Bruce named the company Jazz Pharmaceuticals. Obviously jazz

musicians are very talented individually, but the beauty of jazz is when you have talented soloists come together and make music that is greater than the sum of its parts.

This value comes from the top. The Jazz executive committee, which is a group of senior executives, makes decisions about the strategic and day-to-day operations of the company in a collaborative way. It's a discussion about, "What's the right decision for us here? Let's weigh the risks, let's get an expert in to talk to us about the law or the regulation, and let's make an educated decision together as to what's the right outcome." I think we try to drive consensus as much as possible. It's not always possible—eventually someone has to make a decision—but we try to make sure decisions aren't made in silos to eliminate some of that risk and arrive at the best outcome.

The Green Visor: Not Exactly a Superhero

Many business cultures are not collaborative in nature. Often the work of an accountant is pretty isolating. The image of an accountant as a little man wearing a green visor, working alone over his ledgers is somewhat accurate.

Salespeople and production people often view the bean counters with disdain and fear that accountants might screw up the numbers and cost them money. Clearly, they want the accounting department to turn out numbers that make them look good. Following the accounting rules is not especially important to them.

Many accountants do not have the outgoing personality to be in operations or sales and may not be particularly confrontational by nature. This of course plays into the hand of the very assertive CEO who wants his accountants to always produce numbers that help the bottom line.

*"It's up to you now, Miller. The only thing that can save us
is an accounting breakthrough."*

Accounting in the Real World

College teaches that accounting should produce reports representing the true financial picture of the company. You are taught not to work backwards or decide in advance what you want the numbers to be. You are taught that it's not okay to change your accounting methods just because they do not produce the desired results.

Then you get out of college and discover the real world of business. Holy cow! Almost no one in the business world is impressed or motivated by pristine accounting methods. Over time (and it doesn't take long), you learn that in many company cultures, advancing in your career means producing good numbers.

Ask any accountant after several years in the real world. She is likely to tell you that she has been asked to make the numbers look better by one or more of these actions:

- Avoiding reporting taxable income
- Changing accounting methods to improve the bottom line
- Not making material entries to the books
- Putting lipstick on the pig when presenting numbers to Wall Street, commercial banks and/or employees

Upper management outside of the accounting department knows that "generally acceptable accounting" is often not black or white. There are lots of grey areas. Accrual accounting requires a great deal of estimating to recognize revenue and expenses when incurred regardless of when cash is received or disbursed. The more assets on the balance sheet that are subject to change in assumption and forecast, the greater the manager's flexibility to manage short-term earnings.

An article in *CFO Magazine* discusses "suspect accounting."

In a recent study, a group of nearly 400 CFOs said they believe that in a given period, one-fifth of companies are distorting earnings—that is, following the letter of generally accepted accounting principles but not necessarily the spirit. They also said that on average, the earnings distortion is as large as 10 cents on every dollar of earnings.

About 60% of these accountants felt that the distortion would likely go undetected. Some CFOs even thought it could take up to five years for anyone to uncover the sleight of hand. Indeed the accounting frauds at Enron, HealthSouth, World-Com, and others lasted about seven years before coming to light.

A number of academic studies verify that CFOs are often pressured by the CEO to manipulate the numbers. The findings suggest that CFOs are typically not the instigator of accounting manipulations. Instead, it appears that CEOs—especially powerful CEOs with high equity incentives—exert significant influence over a CFO's financial reporting decisions.

In other words, pressure from a CEO often compromises the CFO's role as the watchdog over financial reports.

One such study suggested a need for corporate governance reform. And, while stock-based compensation incentives can tempt a CFO to misstate accounting numbers, redesigning those compensation packages isn't the only potential remedy. What if you could give a CFO more independence by alleviating pressure from the CEO? One possible way to achieve this would be to have boards or audit committees more involved in CFO performance evaluation and in hiring and retention decisions.

ETHICAL PLAY #13

"The grey areas of accounting often give birth to fraud."

The general public has very little understanding of the role that "estimating" plays in accounting. In fact, with the exception of cash and land, all assets on the balance sheet are based on estimates. These are the grey areas.

Sometimes, fraud begins the moment an estimate is changed to achieve a bottom line number.

Sometimes You Have to Cut Your Losses

But this isn't a book about organizational reform. It's about you and me working in the real world and learning to make the right decisions—not just because they are right for the company, but also because they are the right thing to do.

Sometimes in that real world, whether you are the CFO or just one of the bean counters, the pressure from management becomes too much. If you are being pushed too hard to make the numbers and you know you can't do it ethically, it's time to either speak out, leave the job, or both. You may be job hunting, but at least your conscience will be clear. There are other positions out there for an honest bean counter.

Marianne Jennings provides a hopeful perspective: "My students are very driven. They think, 'I've got to get my college degree, then my master's degree. I've got to get a good job and I'll be fine.' Actually, you won't. You're going to have a lot of challenges in life and there is a good likelihood you will lose your job in some of these situations. But if you're hardworking, capable, and bright, you're going to be fine. You will land on your feet."

CHAPTER 14

Short Term Gains Can Be Our Loss

The key success secret for credit card companies is the natural bias humans have toward short-term instant gratification. They make a lot of money by catering to this bias. Two MIT professors, for instance, conducted an auction of Boston Celtics tickets as a social experiment, telling half the participants they had to pay with cash and the other half they had to pay with credit cards. After averaging the bids for the two groups, they found that the average credit card bid was twice as high as the average cash bid!

Many credit card users fall victim to short-term thinking. The credit card companies will tell you the least profitable customer is one who pays their bill off every month and never incurs a late fee.

Banks and credit card companies are currently mailing out over five billion separate pieces of mail each year promoting their cards. I receive a handful of such mail every week. The advertising for these cards convey to people that they can take their dream vacation TODAY, own that new big screen TV TODAY and, in general, live the life they have always dreamed about with the bank's credit card.

This is not a sustainable business model. There are probably no laws being broken. The banks can surely say, "If the American people want these loans we should make them available. There is a demand for our product and we are meeting that demand." But in the long run does it make sense? After the fallout of the Great Recession we finally realized it was not socially responsible to make home loans to people who could not afford the debt.

Free Cigarettes to All Students

When I was a college student during the early 1960s, the tobacco companies gave students free cigarettes outside the student union. Today, the large banks distribute high interest credit cards to students close to graduation. The tobacco companies wanted students to start smoking and hopefully develop a lifelong habit. Today, the banks hope for the same type of outcome: a lifelong addiction to debt. The fact that very few people of influence seem to be concerned about this business practice is troubling. It is my belief that this unsustainable behavior may result in something similar to the subprime debacle. Before it blew up, not much was being said until it was too late.

Our addiction to short-term gains can be dangerous in the world of business. We have to resist the urge to let society, the media, Wall Street and other forces lure us into the false security of short-term thinking.

ETHICAL PLAY #14

"Making money for the long run depends on ethics."

Wall Street pressures public companies to deliver quarterly profits. This emphasis on the short term is part of human nature. We simply value what we have today more than what we might have in the future. This pressure often results in unethical behavior. In the long run, profits will suffer if this happens. Ethical behavior today will bear more fruit in the future than will unethical practices.

CHAPTER 15

Sociopathic or Just Manipulative?

I was watching the Today Show one morning in 2003, after the HealthSouth fraud had made the news. Huge corporate frauds were front-page fodder. The topic of discussion for the show that day was, "What type of person can commit such frauds?" There was a panel of experts, including a clinical psychologist, discussing the subject. After listing various examples of recent frauds, the psychologist pointed out that in many cases the person at the center might be a sociopath. I had more than a passing interest in what he had to say.

In my efforts to better understand sociopaths, I discovered Dr. Martha Stout's book, *The Sociopath Next Door*. The first eye-opening statement in her book is that as many as one in 25 people may actually be a sociopath.

Emotional Sirens

When I tell other people this statistic, most find it hard to believe. One reason for that might be that many people think of a sociopath as a cold-blooded killer such as those depicted as the TV show, "Criminal Minds." The truth is the sociopath can come in many forms with different levels of intelligence, ambition, and proclivity for violence. The key thing that all sociopaths have in common is that they have little or no conscience. To quote from Dr. Stout's book: "It is not that this group fails to grasp the difference between good and bad; it is that the distinction fails to limit their behavior. The intellectual difference between right and wrong does not bring on the emotional sirens and flashing blue lights or the fear of God that it does for the rest of us. One in 25 people can do anything at all."

When we talk about cheating and lying in business, the sociopath pushes the extreme end of the spectrum. You, dear reader, probably aren't one, and you wouldn't admit it if you were. (In her book, Dr. Stout asks, "Do sociopaths know they are sociopaths?" Her answer is that a sociopath can read her book from cover to cover and fail to see himself depicted.) The important thing, though, is that sociopathic behavior is much more common than most of us realize. If the statistics are right, it is certain that during your life you will have to deal with one of them. In fact, you may work for one of them.

Real Charmers

The sociopath may be very intelligent and ambitious with a desire to be wealthy and powerful. In this case, a career in business, politics, law, banking or any array of power professions would be a nice fit. The lack of conscience gives the sociopath a big advantage over others in these professions, as it frees him of many normal restraints. The sociopath often is enabled by his ability to superficially charm and to seduce others with his charisma. He is probably more spontaneous, or more intense, or more complex, or sexier, or more entertaining than everyone else. However, he rarely has a trace of empathy.

On the other hand, the sociopath may not be that intelligent and really does not want much of anything. His real ambition is not to have to exert himself to get by. He does not want to work like everyone else. The sociopath learns how to live off of others like relatives and friends. Often he will get into a sexual relationship (with no true love) and sponge off the other person.

Of course, there *are* cold-blooded killer sociopaths. Thank goodness there are far fewer of them than the non-violent types.

Sociopaths are infamous for their refusal to acknowledge responsibility for their decisions or the outcomes of those decisions. Instead, when confronted with a destructive outcome, they will deny responsibility and, to all appearances, believe their own lie. This feature of the sociopath makes self-awareness impossible. Just as the sociopath has no genuine relationships with others, he has only a very tenuous one with himself. Thinking himself superior to others, he almost never seeks professional help. Why should he? He's one of the good guys.

The Perfect Economic Animal

Dan Ariely is aware of my experience at HealthSouth since I've been honored to speak to his students at Duke University. I asked him about sociopathic leaders. Here's what he said:

> Sociopaths are basically the perfect economic animals, right? They are people who, in principle, just have some objective and they have no morals in the way. They know what they want and they do everything to get there. They basically do the cost-benefit analysis: they think about whether they can get what they want, what are the costs, will they get caught, and so on.

> Look, I don't doubt that sociopaths exist, but the fact is that we have ways to identify sociopaths, and we have ways to deal with them. I think the whole legal system is already set up for them, so if we improved a little bit how we deal with sociopaths, I don't think we would do much better.

> On the other hand, I think the type of dishonesty I talk about is one we don't think about much and aren't set up to deal with, and that's people who are *not* sociopaths. It's hard to look at all the corporate fraud and basically ask: how much of it is due to people who are sociopaths and how much of it is due to some kind of slippery slope? What we would have to do from my perspective is to look at (this person) in the early days and basically say, "Is this a sociopath? Has he always been like this in all of his

companies or did he also have a slippery slope that started way before he met you?" Maybe it started at a younger age. Would he also cheat at poker? You could ask all kinds of questions. And I think, yes, there are some evil people out there that are full sociopaths, but I think we give this disease or these personality traits too much weight and we don't understand sufficiently the nature of how people can progress and become worse and worse over time because their morality just deteriorates.

Know Thyself

In *Snakes in Suits,* Dr. Paul Babiak and Dr. Robert Hare suggest that the best defense against sociopathic manipulation is to learn all you can about this type of person and their nature. The authors, like Ariely, also point out that the term *sociopath* has many negative connotations, and that careless application of the label would be unfair. I agree. But when it comes to dealing with (especially working for) someone who even *resembles* a sociopath, I suggest you follow the wise woodman's credo: "Assume a snake is poisonous until you can prove otherwise." This will help you make the decision whether to distance yourself from the person in question.

You should also learn all you can about yourself. Self-knowledge will strengthen your immunity against sociopaths or any kind of manipulator. Sociopaths feed on what they see as naiveté and innocence. In effect, a perceptive sociopath may know you better than you know yourself. The more you know who you are, the better able you will be to defend against manipulation.

I learned this lesson the hard way. I now clearly realize I am not a very confrontational person. Given the chance of getting into a fight or just walking away, I usually chose the latter. This, of course, can be good and bad. Manipulative people have learned this about me and used it against me.

Marianne Jennings' advice to her students is on target. "I

ETHICAL PLAY #15

"People rationalize unethical behavior so they can live with themselves."

Normal people feel bad about themselves when they knowingly do wrong. They often try to feel better by rationalizing their bad behavior.

tell them there are three components (to understanding ethical behavior). One is to understand your thinking process, one is to understand the company culture and what it can do to you, and the third is *you*—deciding who you are, deciding what you will do and won't do. And not defining yourself by the car, the house, and those kinds of things."

PART THREE:
A PLAYBOOK FOR YOUR
PERSONAL SUCCESS

CHAPTER 16

Learning Ethics Early

Not too long ago, I gave a speech at the Altamont School in Birmingham, a fine college preparatory school for fifth-graders through high-school graduates. I enjoy speaking to student audiences, and I've respected Altamont for years. This sentence on its website might explain why its administrators were willing to hire a speaker to come and talk about ethics: "The Altamont experience encourages students to think critically, communicate truthfully and live honorably."

One of the audience members was 16-year-old Sarah Polhill. She loves writing and playing violin in the youth orchestra. She also participates in the honor court, a panel of faculty members and student judges. When a student is caught cheating or has committed some other academic violation, the honor court tries to decide the best consequence and way to support the student after the event.

Recently, the producer of a video about my work interviewed this remarkable young woman. I think her views about ethical behavior are on point. She said:

> When students come forward and turn themselves in or are completely open about what they did and are basically telling us everything and being very truthful about it, it really speaks a lot about that person because we're all subject to making mistakes. What they choose to do after they've been caught or after they've turned themselves in says a lot about their character, too.
>
> What makes me really sad is when kids come in, and we

have evidence that shows that they've done something wrong but they still lie about it. That just makes me really sad because we need to have that conscience that says this is wrong, and listen to that feeling we have before we do something wrong—that feeling that tells us, "Don't do this. This is wrong." And too often, we just ignore it.

Recognizing the Line

Sarah and her classmates are learning about honest dealings and ethical behavior at a young age, as they should. They are learning to be accountable for their behavior. As American high-schoolers, however, I fear they are in the minority.

Professor Marianne Jennings, who at Arizona State teaches young people who are five to 10 years older than Sarah and her peers, confronts what she calls, "60 years of moral relativism," in her classroom every day. Many of her students, in other words, act and speak as though their goal (whatever that might be) is the only important thing, and how you get there isn't the issue. She calls them self-definers. "They self-define what is okay and what is not okay, according to the goal. So they might say, 'this is just a stupid required class so if I cheat, big deal.' So you've got to get them out of the idea that everything is grey back to a brighter, clearer line."

You might think that Jennings introducing the idea of right and wrong in a business setting might shock the students' systems. But just the opposite seems to be true. "I have a great deal of hope," she says, "[because] once they start thinking about it in a different way, there's a sense of relief about it. They're very relieved to think, 'Wait a minute. I can have some rules, it can be pretty clear. I don't have to worry about any landmines going off. I can live a principled life. I can do this.'"

That's a relief for me to hear because the students in these classrooms are tomorrow's leaders, accountants, and employees. The more ethical education they get, the better the chances

ETHICAL PLAY #16

**"What is right is right, even
when no one is doing it."**

are that, in matters small and large, they will recognize that "brighter, clearer line" when it matters most.

Recognizing Good Ethics

While most universities now teach ethics in their business schools, few high schools offer any training with ethical behavior as a main focus. I believe ethics programs can be started at the high school level, and these programs can be very beneficial in getting young people off to a good start in building ethical strength.

In 2013, I joined the Rotary Club in Robertsdale, Alabama. Although I'm on the road speaking a lot, I try to attend as many weekly Rotary lunch meetings as possible. Through Rotary, I've met a lot of good folks who do good work in their communities. Guinn Massey, from Little Rock, Arkansas, is one of them.

One of Rotary International's guiding purposes is to encourage high ethical standards in all vocations. Guinn wanted to do something at the high school level to recognize students who had demonstrated outstanding ethical behavior in the past year. Twenty years ago, his Rotary chapter starting selecting four high schools in the Little Rock area to launch the program. Guinn asked the school's principal and teachers to select two students, a boy and a girl, who stood out as ethical students. The schools were asked to select students who were not necessarily star athletes, homecoming queens, or valedictorians.

One of the students selected was a seventh grader who, on the first day back from Christmas break, found a wallet on the floor at school. It didn't have the owner's name in it, but did include some cash and gift cards—probably the young owner's Christmas presents. The finder did the right thing by turning in the wallet to the principal, who located the owner.

Another young man, a football player who had cheated on an important test and realized he had done wrong, reported it to his teacher. The teacher warned him that he would receive a failing grade and be removed from the football team for a period of time. The player said he understood, but that he wanted to do the right thing.

Young people like these are featured at a special Rotary Club meeting near the end of the school year. In front of parents, grandparents, and other family members, the students are recognized and receive a plaque and a check for $100. Just think if every Rotary Club (32,000 total) had selected eight students for such an award each year for the past 20 years. There would now be more than five million more people walking around with the knowledge that intentionally ethical behavior is worthwhile.

Guinn, a retired CPA who travels the country speaking to Rotary chapters, told me the program continues to this day, has received a lot of attention in the local media, and is a favorite event for his club members.

For the most part, I believe that people—from students to someone in the latter part of their career—know ethical from unethical behavior. What they have to learn and practice is *how* to be ethical. They need to be trained.

CHAPTER 17

Developing Ethical Strength

Building ethical strength is an ongoing process. Just as athletes must practice to improve their playing ability, people in business must also practice building ethical strength. You cannot take a couple of golf lessons to learn the basic strokes and declare yourself a good golfer—you must hit the golf ball thousands of times to become good at the game. Some medical research suggests that surgeons who do a high volume of a particular surgery have better outcomes than doctors who only occasionally do the same surgery.

During my business career, while I realized ethics was important, I did little to build my ethical strength. I would back away from voicing my values. Dr. Mary Gentile, in her book, *Giving Voice to Values*, explains that voicing your values is a competency that can be learned. You are more likely to voice your values if you practice how to respond to frequently encountered conflicts. You will become fluent in ways to address the defenses of less ethical behaviors. Like an athlete develops muscle memory through practice, we can avoid the deer-in-headlights feeling when we confront values conflicts.

Sully Saves the Day

If practicing for ethical conflicts is at all similar to preparing for flight emergencies, a lot can be learned from Chesley "Sully" Sullenberger.

On January 15, 2009, Captain Sullenberger landed US Airways Flight 1549 in the Hudson River in New York City. There was no loss of life. To me, this was a bigger accomplishment than winning the Super Bowl or flying to the moon. Let me repeat. He landed a jet airplane filled with 155 souls on a river in the middle of New York City without engines running. Later, it was discovered that the airplane had become disabled when it struck a flock of Canadian geese during its takeoff from LaGuardia Airport.

Captain Sullenberger, without knowing it, had been in training for this event for decades. During his 40 years and 20,000 hours of flying experience, he studied every major airplane crash and ditched-water landing. He helped with many accident investigations conducted by the Air Force and the National Transportation Safety Board. He was instrumental in developing and implementing the Crew Resource Management course that is used by US Airways. He has taught the course to hundreds of airline crewmembers. Sullenberger also studied the psychology behind keeping an airline crew functioning during a crisis. In a CBS *60 Minutes* interview, he told anchor Katie Couric, "One way of looking at this might be that for 42 years, I've been making small, regular deposits in this bank of experience, education, and training. And on January 15 the balance was sufficient so that I could make a very large withdrawal."

When Birds Fly Into Your Engine

When I am speaking to college students, I tell them about Captain Sullenberger. They need to know what to do when birds fly into *their* engine. It will happen.

Training to develop ethical skill, ethical muscle—whatever you want to call it—makes sense. Think about it. If you are hired to work in a factory, you are given safety training before you begin work. This is to help you avoid causing injury to yourself or others. Smart employers continue that training on a regular basis. Students must realize there are ethical dangers in the business world just as there are physical dangers in a factory.

Coaches train their players to seek perfection. They realize no team or player will be able to play a perfect game. But they train for that goal. Why?

I think St. Augustine (354 to 430 AD) said it best as it relates to ethical behavior. "Complete abstinence is easier than perfect moderation." In other words, when training for ethical behavior, complete abstinence from unethical behavior should be the goal. Do not lie *ever*. Do not cheat or steal *at all*. Dr. Ariely points out that we all have a tendency to cheat a little, but *aiming* for a level of moderate cheating? That's an invitation to eventual disaster. No football coach tells his players before the season starts, "Men, I'm going to train you to play this game moderately well." There is no way of defining that concept. No signposts. Talk about grey areas!

Think of it in these terms. What if you drink too much? Maybe you aren't an alcoholic, but drinking has caused you some personal and professional problems. The obvious way to fix your problem (and to avoid a bigger one in the future) is to drink zero alcohol. Otherwise, how do you know you are drinking at a moderately correct level?

We must try to live our lives as ethically as possible. How much do we want to be lied to or cheated by others? Zero. What is the perfect level of texting while you are driving? Zero. Things are not as grey as we like to make them.

Getting a Handle on Rationalizations

I usually end my speeches with the St. Augustine quote from above. One day, during the Q and A session, a college student stood up and asked me, "But Mr. Beam, aren't there grey areas in business where being perfect really doesn't work?" I told him that there are at least 50 shades of grey. That usually gets a laugh from the audience. But, I continued, if you're not careful you'll tend to see and define things as grey so you can rationalize your own unethical behavior. If you really study the situation you'll see that it's probably much more black and white

ETHICAL PLAY #17

"What is wrong is wrong, even if everyone is doing it.

than grey. You should look for the solution that is as close as possible to "complete abstinence" from unethical behavior.

It's easier to make the right decisions when you have a handle on your rationalizations. As Dr. Ariely points out, virtually all humans have the capacity to do certain dishonest things without damaging their self-concept as honest. Unfettered rationalization leads us down a slippery slope, leading us to lie to just about everyone—including ourselves—to cover for our unethical behavior. The road to stopping this vicious cycle starts with recognizing the rationalizations—and hearing ourselves invoking them—and immediately realizing that it is time to rethink the decision.

In the long run, you'll never regret taking the high road. If you compromise your personal values—assuming honesty and integrity are among them—in small things, you will eventually do so in larger things.

Seeing decision points in black and white and acting on them isn't always the popular or easy choice, but it's doable. "I think that anybody has a choice no matter what the situations of the world are and how difficult it will be," said Sarah Polhill. "I definitely believe that oftentimes making an ethical decision will put someone at a disadvantage. But it's a disadvantage they have to accept and choose if they want to be ethical."

I know. It's easy to say and hard to do. But with practice it becomes easier.

The Four-Way Test

At the beginning of every weekly Rotary meeting we recite the Four-Way Test, a way to determine "the right thing" in what we say and how we live.

1. Is it the TRUTH?
2. Is it FAIR to all concerned?
3. Will it build GOODWILL and BETTER FRIENDSHIPS?

4. Will it be BENEFICIAL to all concerned?

Developing the habit of considering the consequences of your decisions is one of the ways to build ethical strength.

There's Power in Ethics

I have a friend who used to work for an audiobook publisher in Chicago. The company would take self-help books and turn them into cassettes and later, compact discs. They sold them by the hundreds of thousands. He told me about his work as a producer, converting these books—some from world-famous authors and speakers and others from literary rookies—into the audio format. He told me how important it was to condense big ideas into nuggets, bullet points, and sound bites for the listening consumer. Even some of the titles suggested a tidy, convenient solution to a problem. You know, the "10 Power Tips" for this and the "25 Power Tactics" for that. My friend told me that having the word "power" in the title would almost guarantee a top seller.

There *is* power in being ethical. You don't have to live with shame. You don't have to "keep your story straight" because of the lies you've told. You can expect the best out of people because they expect the best out of you.

That being said, I still don't have a power list for you for building and sustaining ethical muscle in your life and career. It's work. It's listening and watching and knowing who you are. It's putting actions to your values. It's making independent judgments about your decisions and not becoming part of the groupthink squad.

If You Can Trust Yourself

Even though I don't have a list, three ideas jumped from the pages of a poem I was recently introduced to.

Keep your head.

Trust yourself.
Don't deal in lies.

The poem is called "If" and was written by Englishman Rudyard Kipling in 1895. Another big idea from that poem is this: *Make allowance for the shortcomings of others.* As Sarah Polhill said:

> One of the major things I've learned, especially serving on the honor court, is that everybody, no matter their background, no matter their beliefs, is subject to making an ethical mistake. You have to continually watch yourself. It can't just be, "Oh, okay, I'm never going to do that. I'm not worrying about it." You have to go through every day of your academic career keeping that decision to be an honorable person in mind. I think once you're raised for years with something, even if you stray from it, you always kind of go back to it, especially when it's something good and it's something that speaks to your conscience and you know it's right.

No matter what you have done in your past, it's never too late to start developing the practice of good ethical decision making.

> If
> by Rudyard Kipling
>
> If you can keep your head when all about you
> Are losing theirs and blaming it on you,
> If you can trust yourself when all men doubt you,
> But make allowance for their doubting too;
> If you can wait and not be tired by waiting,
> Or being lied about, don't deal in lies,
> Or being hated, don't give way to hating,
> And yet don't look too good, nor talk too wise:
>
> If you can dream—and not make dreams your master;
> If you can think—and not make thoughts your aim;

If you can meet with Triumph and Disaster
And treat those two impostors just the same;
If you can bear to hear the truth you've spoken
Twisted by knaves to make a trap for fools,
Or watch the things you gave your life to, broken,
And stoop and build 'em up with worn-out tools:

If you can make one heap of all your winnings
And risk it on one turn of pitch-and-toss,
And lose, and start again at your beginnings
And never breathe a word about your loss;
If you can force your heart and nerve and sinew
To serve your turn long after they are gone,
And so hold on when there is nothing in you
Except the Will which says to them: 'Hold on!'

If you can talk with crowds and keep your virtue,
Or walk with Kings—nor lose the common touch,
If neither foes nor loving friends can hurt you,
If all men count with you, but none too much;
If you can fill the unforgiving minute
With sixty seconds' worth of distance run,
Yours is the Earth and everything that's in it,
And—which is more—you'll be a Man, my son!

Eternal Vigilance

Even the best-intentioned businessperson can find it difficult
to stay on the straight and narrow. Even if we avoid serious
temptation, crooked bosses, and corner-cutting colleagues, we
still are apt to frame problems and make decisions that might
look unethical. The higher the stakes and the more complex the
business transactions, the greater the potential that negative
pressures will influence the decisions we make. Is following a
system of moral absolutes the answer? Many strong leaders say

they follow such a code but have problems doing so. Religious leaders are often caught in unethical situations. Moral absolutes such as those found in the Bible can be interpreted in many ways and often don't address complex modern business situations.

Is education the answer? Learning ethical standards in high school and college is very important to a successful career but often the disconnect between the rose-colored glasses worn in an ethics class and the harsh light of business reality is too much to take.

While moral reminders and education are important elements to maintaining an ethical business life, I think the secret is what Professor Jennings calls "eternal vigilance."

To me, that means thinking about ethics every day and in every way. Robert Prentice says that more people accidentally back into ethical problems than make a truly conscious decision to turn to a life of wrongdoing. "Simple as it sounds," he says, "there remains no better technique than to think, every day: 'What would my mom say about the decisions I am making today if she were to read about them in the newspapers tomorrow?'"

Applying courage is also required—sometimes more than a little—especially when we have to stand up to colleagues and supervisors. There is research on people who have acted courageously—European civilians who helped shelter Jews in World War II, for instance—that indicates these people had pre-scripted themselves to act in such a way. In other words, they had thought in advance about how they would act in such a circumstance and, when the situation arose, they merely acted in a way they had scripted for themselves.

Maybe this is what ethics education (whether in the classroom or in the "school of hard knocks") does: giving us the chance to practice making ethical decisions in real-world situations. Prentice claims, and I agree, that, "Simply thinking about such ethical pitfalls in advance and considering a proper course of action should dramatically improve the odds that people will do the right thing."

CHAPTER 18

Is There an Ethical Core?

Marianne Jennings told me that research shows about a third of today's students have a basic understanding of ethics, so they go into the workplace "outnumbered." She continues, "I see this in my classes, too, about a third have a very strong sense of ethics, whether they've gotten it from home or church. As the term goes on, they'll be more definitive in their answers, so you can tell they've gotten it somewhere. And if you talk to them, they can all point to an experience (when they were younger) where they did something wrong and someone who they knew loved them, and whom they respected, made them make it right. There's something about that accountability and respect that builds moral behavior."

Holding a child accountable for his or her misdeeds is important, but no parent gets it right every time. It's difficult work. Parents want the moral values they teach (and, hopefully, practice) to stick with their children into adulthood, and that's one of the reasons some parents try to get their children involved in church at a young age. The Bible contains the best "power" bullet points for business ethics ever conceived: the Ten Commandments. But the Good Book is also filled with morality stories that even children can grasp, if properly presented and modeled.

That Golden Rule

Values vary from culture to culture, but there is one universally recognized axiom that, if followed, can lead to living a truly ethical life: *Do unto others as you would have them do unto you.*

This Golden Rule is also referred to as the ethic of reciprocity. In Walter Terence Stace's 1937 book, *The Concept of Morals*, he argues that the Golden Rule is much more than simply an ethical code. Instead, he says, it "expresses the essence of a universal morality." Variations of the rule are found in a wide range of world cultures and religions including Confucianism, Hinduism, Buddhism, Taoism, Christianity, Existentialism, Islam, Judaism, and Scientology.

However, in some cultures there are culturally ingrained practices that fly in the face of the Golden Rule. Take bribery, for instance.

Paying off a government official or businessperson—to gain access to markets, to cross a nation's border, to procure a contract for services, or countless other reasons—is participating in a type of extortion. In extortion, the implication is, "If you don't pay me what I demand, something bad is going to happen." Yet the culture of bribery is entrenched in countries around the world. Some companies working internationally even budget for it. A friend of mine was crossing the border from Hungary several years ago on mission trip with 50 other church members. Their bus driver had to pay a bribe to the border guard in order to enter Romania. That was standard operating procedure. It was an "acceptable" part of the culture.

What's the ethical thing to do? Well, the first thing, and it's a no-brainer, is to never put yourself in a position to *ask* someone for a bribe. If one is demanded of you, all I can say is resist wherever and however you can. I may be old-fashioned, but I am optimistic that, in the long run, goodness will prevail against evil. It starts with individuals who act in an honorable and ethical way.

My Religion

During the Q and A, I am often asked questions like, "Are you a Christian?" "Do you belong to a church?" Answering these questions has always been awkward for me because for most of my life I have not attended church. I assumed that the people asking these questions were thinking, "Ah, *there* is the problem. If Mr. Beam had been a good Christian, he would not have committed this huge fraud."

During the years after the HealthSouth fraud was exposed, Phyllis and I had some very difficult moments. Phyllis is a cradle Catholic and has done a good job practicing her faith. During the darkest years of our more than four decades of marriage, I noticed that she really leaned on her Catholic upbringing for help. She began never missing church. Often I would find her by the bed praying, sometimes with tears in her eyes. This really impacted me. I could see the hurt I had caused her and I felt about six inches tall.

So I took the first step. I told her I wanted to attend church (St. Margaret Catholic Church) with her one week a month. I felt I needed to share what she was experiencing. This was probably in 2006 after I had gotten out of prison. At first I would keep looking at my watch during the service, hoping the time would pass faster. However, over time I started to enjoy my monthly obligation. I especially liked Father Paul Zoghby. His homilies were very well done and I began to learn a lot about the church, the Bible and the history of religion.

By now, some members of the church were getting to know me and were asking me to consider joining the church. One dear lady, Cordy, was really twisting my arm in a nice way but I could tell she was on a mission to win me over. In 2011, Phyllis suggested I attend the RCIA (Rite of Christian Initiation of Adults) classes taught once a week by Father Zoghby. The classes are for both church members and nonmembers who want to learn more about the Catholic church, what Catholics believe, how they celebrate in the sacraments, how to live that belief through the commandments, and how to live a life of prayer through faith.

I was amazed at what a good teacher Father Zoghby is and, I'm glad to say, I only missed two classes because of my speaking engagements.

About midway into the classes, I found myself seriously thinking about joining the church. Over several weeks I went back and forth trying to decide if I would join. Toward the end of the classes I met with Father and told him what I was trying to decide. I explained that I was afraid that joining the church was just to please Phyllis. We discussed it and I came to the conclusion that it might not be such a bad idea. I realized at that moment it would be a process. For instance, during a class one night, Father told us not to join the church if we could not make a commitment to attend mass every week. I am happy to say that, in my first two years as a Catholic, I have not failed in my commitment.

Phyllis cried when I told her I was going to be confirmed a Catholic. It was a special moment in our lives and I only hope I can keep improving the way I live.

Priest or FBI?

My first confession was very trying. I have since joked that it lasted three days and I had to have a lawyer present. I did tell Father that confessing to a priest was a lot better than confessing to the FBI. The FBI agent did not say my sins would be forgiven. He told me I was going to prison.

What is the point of my sharing this with you? If everyone joined a church, would unethical business behavior go away? Of course not. But if everybody abided by commandments number eight (do not steal), number nine (do not lie) and number 10 (do not desire anything that does not belong to you), we wouldn't have any ethical problems. The parallel between those three commandments and ethical behavior is undeniable. It's just so hard for humans to follow these rules!

I realize this is all very personal. I am not telling you to

ETHICAL PLAY #18

"Conduct yourself ethically in personal life matters."

The obligation of good faith dealings with each other does not change because we are no longer at the office. To keep building our ethical strength, we need to attempt to do the right thing all the time.

start going to church. But in my case, the church is helping me to do this hard work.

Do and Don't Do

Dan Ariely frames the subject in another way:

> We want people to realize the consequences of their actions, to contemplate their morality. I think we need to basically go back to religion and say that what religion does so well is to give people rules for behavior—do and don't do. These are rules that are not "do sometimes and do when it's convenient to do it," or "do it under the right circumstances." It's do and don't do. And those rules of do and don't do are incredibly important and I think we need to have more of those rules.
>
> If you ask me about accounting practices and you say, "Well, I have this general accounting practice of 'do what's in the best interest of my client.'" What does that really mean? How do you interpret it? But if I had a specific rule of what you do and what you don't do, then life would become much simpler and people would not violate to the same degree their own moral considerations.

Joining the Church has helped me connect my words and actions to what AA members call a *higher power*. Ariely talks about a higher *purpose*.

> The other thing is you want to have it (the goal of more ethical living) tied to a higher purpose. So think about something like recycling. If every day you would think about whether you should or shouldn't recycle, there would be many days in which you decide today it's not worth my while. But if you took a different approach and you said recycling is what a good person does, now this

would not be a daily question. You would just buy into the whole endeavor. And I think we need to do the same thing with honesty. We need to say, this is just what people do, this is what good people do and there's no question of what do we do today differently than yesterday.

Honesty and plain dealing as the norm—what a concept! To quote Bob Dylan, "You don't need a weatherman to know which way the wind blows."

CHAPTER 19

Putting Your Ethical Muscle to Work

We like to shop where we feel welcome. It makes us feel better about our purchase because we have confidence in the service provided and the price we pay. Our loyalty to that store is solid. We tell our friends about it. It feels right because it's a good fit.

So why don't more job seekers work harder to seek the right fit in a prospective employer? And, more specifically, why don't job candidates practice due diligence to find out if the company values anything other than revenue numbers? Just as companies screen out job candidates that may be trouble, you might want to do some screening yourself.

Greg Womble, a longtime friend and a collaborator on this book, found himself in a career change several years ago and missed all the warning signs of a bad employment fit. He tells this story:

> I had been screened by HR and it was time for my interview with the key executives. I felt my chances were good and I was very comfortable with the mission of the organization, which was a large, member-driven nonprofit. I knew I could do the work and was kind of giddy at the possibility of finding the right spot for my career skills.
>
> I was ushered into the executive conference room and there sat the president/CEO, a stern-looking woman, surrounded by a half-dozen people without a smile between them. I went around the conference table introducing myself and shaking hands with them, and they all looked kind of surprised, maybe a little fearful. In the meeting, the CEO did

all the talking, except for my responses. I tried to engage the other attendees with eye contact but they mostly looked away or kept their attention on the CEO.

Warning Signals

You might be thinking, "Greg is getting some serious warning signals that this is a lousy fit. The CEO is obviously a command-and-control autocrat. Something is wrong with this culture. Leave the meeting NOW!" But that's not what happened. Greg continues:

> I had read somewhere that it was good to talk with rank and file employees of a company before accepting employment, outside the earshot of whoever is doing the hiring. So I asked the CEO if I could talk with some of her employees and her response was, "Sure," waving her hand across the room at the silent group of executives, "Ask away." Of course, that's not what I had in mind but I didn't push the issue any further. I think I did ask a question or two, and the responses were short and not very helpful. Then I asked the CEO a question about my advancement prospects within the organization: provided I proved myself worthy, what kind of positions might I aspire to in the organization?
>
> I'll never forget the look on her face: a mix of surprise and disdain. "Well," she half-laughed while making sure her underlings were in on the joke, "I guess one day you could try to replace me!" In the few agonizing moments I spent trying to mentally deconstruct that sarcastic comment and figure out how to respond, I looked around and noticed the other executives halfheartedly laughing with the CEO while trying to avoid eye contact with me.

> Looking back on it, *they* probably knew what a bad fit it was for me, but of course, they were under this leader's thumb and were left with little energy for anything, except maybe pity for me.

At that point, Greg admits, he should have thanked them for the opportunity and politely excused himself, but he was blinded by the prospect of a job he thought he would enjoy with an organization that, for the most part, had a terrific reputation and did good work. Instead, he accepted the position. He told me it was 16 of the longest and hardest months he had ever endured on a job.

Knowing yourself and your values is vital to knowing if a business culture is a good fit for you. Just because it's a bad employment fit doesn't necessarily mean it's a crooked company or one with a culture that doesn't emphasize ethical behavior. There are, however, warning signs that you have to observe to increase your chances of landing the right job with a company that values the ethical muscle you've been developing.

How Can I Select an Ethical Company for Employment?

For most of my corporate career I worked for publicly traded companies, so that's my orientation. Hopefully, though, this section will be helpful to anyone who understands how crucial the job selection process is—even in the so-so job economy we've had in the recovery since the 2008 crash.

Certain industries are more prone to unethical behavior than others. Industries that have inherent conflicts of interest—financial firms, for instance—can recognize tremendous financial rewards by bending the rules. Obviously, I am not saying you should avoid such fields, but just be aware that the temptation to make easy money will always be present—especially in companies with a numbers-first mentality.

The interview process can be very important in select-

ETHICAL PLAY #19

"A strong ethical culture helps retain the best employees."

Karla Brandau, a speaker on the subject of team building, says, "The fastest way to alienate the best and the brightest of your workforce is to destroy trust by unethical behaviors."

ing an ethical company. Do not be afraid to ask whatever is on your mind. Let the company know that a career with an ethical company is important to you. Ask questions about departments such as corporate compliance, internal audits, and employee training. If the company does not like you asking such questions then it may not be the career position for you.

Professor Marianne Jennings offers this advice:

> When you're interviewing with a company, what are the signs in the culture? How many times has the CFO turned over in that year? How many times have they restated their earnings with the SEC? As an exercise, my students go out and look into a real company and find out all they can about it. They tell me about the CFO and the CEO and about the firm's financials. All this so they can know what they're getting into, to know where this company is headed. And I always tell them, "Check the parking lot. If it's full of Ferraris and that kind of thing, you've probably got a heck of a cowboy culture going on there."

Cultural Matchmaking

I mentioned that Eric Fink of Jazz Pharmaceuticals is global head of learning and development and employee communications. The second part of his job title, Eric explained, allows him to help drive employee engagement throughout the organization to ensure that the company's values live and breathe across all locations. This involves a transparent approach to communicating openly and effectively with employees throughout the year.

The learning and development role, however, charges him with ongoing personnel training and on-boarding of new hires. What would Eric say to a job seeker who's interested in finding the right cultural fit?

My advice would be to make fit your top priority. If the fit is right, you're going to be happy with the job, you're going to be happy with the paycheck, and you're going to have opportunities to grow and develop. There's no easy way to do that; it takes legwork, and it's about talking to people. Start by talking with the people who are on your interview panel. Continue by trying to network and talk with people who aren't on your interview list, to find out what it's really like to work at their company. Another important strategy is to look for consistencies. Often when we go in to an interview, we focus on giving the right answers, but it's equally important to listen for consistency in how employees describe the company. Ask about the importance of ethics, the importance of the values within the organization. In my mind, there's no shortcut to finding the right fit, but I think your chances of being happy and getting an accurate picture of the job and company are greater if you approach the interview process that way.

Listening to Management

Certainly if the company is publicly held, you should review at least three years of documents filed with the Securities and Exchange Commission. Have any of these documents been resubmitted or reviewed by the Commission? Why? The Q and A sections should be read very carefully to help determine the tone at the top. Company literature and advertising should also be reviewed to help get a feel for the company's values. If possible, try to listen to management's discussion with analysts and investors after an earnings release.

Dr. David Larcker at Stanford's graduate School of Business has been doing research on how you can tell when a CEO might be lying. He points out that Kenneth Lay of Enron told his employees at a time when the company was about to implode, "I think our core business is extremely strong. We have a very strong competitive advantage, of course, we are transferring this very successful business model and approach to a lot of new very large markets globally."

Larcker goes on to say that if speeches are filled with words that are *too* emotionally positive—like "fantastic, superb, outstanding, and excellent"—and it all sounds like a big hype, it probably is. His research also disclosed that lying executives tend to overuse words like "we" and "our team" when they talk about their company. They avoid saying "I."

Larcker and Tayan use a 2008 conference call with Erin Callan, former CFO of Lehman Brothers, as an example of "generic and excessively positive" language used to obscure the company's deteriorating financial position.

In the call, just months before Lehman's collapse, she used the word *great* 14 times, *strong* 24 times and *incredibly* eight times. By contrast, she used the word *challenging* six times and *tough* only once. This had, Larcker and Tayan opined, "the effect of conveying a positive tone without providing specific factual data to support her message."

Looking for Consistency

Through interviewing, listening, observing, checking the parking lot and talking with employees, you have the ability to assess if a position is a good cultural fit for you. Again, it's key to know yourself and what you value.

CHAPTER 20

Staying the Ethical Course in the Workplace

Once you are settled in that job, what should you do if you start seeing hints that possible ethical violations are happening? Marianne Jennings urges us not to make assumptions too quickly.

"There's no such thing as a perfect company, because as long as humans run companies you'll always have issues here and there. The assessment that has to be done is whether or not it is getting out of control. Or is there someone who can still bring it back around? Notice how the company behaves when something unethical percolates up. Do they fire him? Does he stay? How does the company behave in these cases?"

Time to Leave?

We know companies aren't perfect. But let's say you are starting to feel that your values and the company's values are not aligned. You've been in several situations where your supervisor sounds like she expects you to do things you know aren't right, or you've seen unethical actions go unpunished by management. What then?

If you're not willing to be a whistleblower, it may be time to leave. It sounds so simple, but it is not easy to walk away from a well-paying job. Frauds are able to grow to a huge size in part because employees are fearful of losing their jobs. Employees in finance and accounting should have an exit plan on the day they begin a new job. Part of the plan should be to have enough savings to weather the storm until a new job can be secured.

The Thing about Whistleblowers

Whistleblowing is an important part of preventing fraud from occurring and expanding over time. Without whistleblowing, many known frauds could have gone on much longer. Some research gives the average length of corporate frauds to be about seven years. The fraud at HealthSouth, in fact, began in 1996 and was not exposed until 2003—by a whistleblower. In an ACFE report published in 2014, tips from whistleblowers accounted for 40% of the detections of frauds.

One of the problems with whistleblowing is that it has such a terrible connotation. Even as young children, we are taught not to be a tattletale. It just doesn't seem honorable to turn in your friend for wrongdoing. We need to realize, however, that in business, government or other organizational sectors, the true purpose of reporting wrongdoing isn't to inflict punishment. It's to prevent further wrongdoing.

In some cases, the first action an employee should take when he sees another employee doing something unethical is to confront that employee directly. Think of it this way: just as unethical employees can negatively influence other employees, ethical employees can make a positive impact on their coworkers. If the employee ceases his unethical behavior, we have possibly the best outcome. As Barney Fife would say, we have "nipped it in the bud." Chances are good no one will lose his job or go to jail if it is nipped quickly. But what if that doesn't work?

Should You Be a Whistleblower?

This can be a tricky question. A lot of thought and planning should take place before any whistleblower action is taken. You might even want to seek legal counsel before taking action. However, in general you should report wrongdoing. The more serious the infraction (like crimes that will result in physical harm to humans or massive financial losses), the more important that it is reported.

My mentor at Penn State, where I've spoken several times, is Dr. Linda Treviño. She is a Distinguished Professor of Organizational Behavior and Business Ethics in the Smeal College of Business, where she's been on the faculty since 1987. Over the years, she has done pioneering work in the area of ethical leadership.

In her textbook, *Managing Business Ethics: Straight Talk about How to Do It Right*, she includes a step-by-step discussion of how best to blow the whistle.

1. Approach your immediate manager first. You should find out exactly how your company wants issues raised and if there is a special process for doing it. If there is, follow the process to the letter.

2. Discuss the issue with your family.

3. Take it to the next level. If you receive no action, take it to the next level. However, ask your manager to go with you to the next level. This will keep the manager from feeling betrayed and he will view you as a team player. If this is unsuccessful, you'll need to consider going outside your chain of command.

4. Contact your company's ethics officer. Also, find out if your state has special legislation regarding whistleblowing, but it may require you to follow certain procedures to protect yourself. You may choose to go to these officials first, especially if your manager is part of the problem.

Protecting Yourself

It takes a lot of courage to blow the whistle on corporate misconduct. Sadly, internal whistleblowers have not always been treated well by management and other employees. I have to believe that it goes back to the culture portrayed in the movies where a snitch is the lowest form of life. It goes against the macho "cowboy culture" (as Professor Jennings calls it) found at a lot of companies. You could be socially ostracized or lose your job. Even if you leave on your own accord you may not have a glowing recommendation to help your career pursuit. Many whistleblowers are blacklisted in their respective industries, making it impossible to find future work there.

Dodd-Frank and Sarbanes-Oxley are two examples of federal regulations that help protect whistleblowers. Sarbanes requires most large organizations to have reporting systems that allow you to report problems and to do so anonymously. Many state laws also provide substantial protection against retaliation to a whistleblower.

This reminds me of the process Matthew talks about in his Gospel while discussing disputes between people. "First, one tries to persuade on a one-to-one basis, but if this fails, take another one or even two with you, and if that fails, get the community involved."

The spirit of this process should be that we are trying to stop unethical behavior from growing and causing great harm to the company, its employees and stockholders. The primary focus is not to send people to prison. Unfortunately, though, this may happen.

Since the word *whistleblower* has such a bad connotation maybe we should rename it *kibosher*, as in, he or she who puts the kibosh on bad behavior. Whatever you call it, in the long run it is not in our best interest to allow wrongdoing to go unreported. Each employee, to some extent, has a duty to act as a corporate compliance officer for the protection of all.

Financial Reward for Whistleblowing

There is a long history of financially rewarding some whistleblowers. The IRS whistleblower program is most notable.

ETHICAL PLAY #20

"Remember the freedom of not being haunted by a falsehood."

After retiring from HealthSouth, I was haunted by what I had done. For several years, every time the doorbell rang, I thought it might be the FBI. I drank more than I should have. Only after admitting my guilt, going to prison, and publicly speaking about my crime has my desire to drink decreased to an appropriate level. I can't help believe there is not a correlation.

The IRS has had a program dating back to 1980, but the 2006 Tax Relief and Health Care Act, greatly increased the maximum payouts. Under the False Claims Act, whistleblowers can collect between 15 and 30 percent of the proceeds recovered. Sometimes the windfall can be huge. Jim Alderson collected over $20 million after he reported that the hospital he worked for had asked him to maintain two sets of books. One set of books contained falsified numbers to be used for Medicare reimbursement and the other set was only for the hospital's use. He sued Quorum Health Group, Inc. and Columbia/HCA under a *qui tam* action.

However, with the median whistleblower award at only $150,000 after legal fees, the financial incentive of whistleblowing almost never outweighs the mental and professional anguish it causes. Still, it's often the right thing to do.

PART FOUR: A PLAYBOOK FOR YOUR ORGANIZATION'S SUCCESS

CHAPTER 21

Mission and Values: Just Buzzwords?

Legend has it that a bookkeeper was denied a $100 monthly raise by his company. The bookkeeper was incensed, so he methodically stole for the next 20 years, until he retired. His replacement discovered an amazing fact: the retired book-keeper had pilfered exactly $100 a month—the precise sum of the raise he had requested.

Now I don't know what kind of company that was—probably a rotten one if the poor guy couldn't get a raise in 20 years. I don't condone his theft, but I can imagine that the bookkeeper might have felt unimportant and uninvolved in the big picture of the organization—even detached from the organization's values, if any were stated. Maybe he noticed the president taking elaborate vacations on the company's dime. Maybe the good old boys who sucked up to the president were the only ones who got a promotion. Maybe the company cheated its customers or vendors. Whatever it was, there was a culture problem at that company.

When I speak to corporate audiences, this little saying usually gets a nervous laugh. "When hiring, you want to look for three things: integrity, intelligence, and drive. If, after you've hired the person, you discover he lacks integrity, you had better hope that he's stupid and lazy, too."

In this final section of the book we'll discuss examples of how a better ethical culture can be built into organizations so disasters like my corporate fraud experience (and bitter employees stealing money) will occur less often. When a company applies *values* to its *mission* and tries to live them out throughout the organization, life is better for everybody. Employees are definitely better off because they can actually trust management (no, this isn't a misprint). Trust builds loyalty. Even when management has to do distasteful things like layoffs and budget cuts, employees can maintain the assurance that the core of the organization is solid.

Wages in Kind

Another thing about employee loyalty: it reduces worker fraud and other misdeeds. Over 30 years ago, a Hollinger and Clark study of 12,000 employees in the workforce found that the most common reason employees committed fraud had little to do with opportunity, but more with motivation. The more dissatisfied the employee, the more likely he or she was to engage in criminal behavior. One criminologist described the phenomenon as "wages in kind." All of us have a sense of our own worth; if we believe we are not being fairly treated or adequately compensated, statistically we are at much higher risk of trying to balance the scales. This gets back to Dr. Ariely's research on cheating: our human nature lets us cheat by only a little bit while still viewing ourselves as good people. This balancing act is the process of rationalizing.

Putting Your Values Out There

In 2013, Jazz Pharmaceuticals was named Fortune's Fastest Growing Company. But instead of trumpeting it from the rooftops, Jazz kept mostly mum about it. We asked Eric Fink about this.

> Interestingly, when we found out about the award and looked at the criteria it involved, we realized that all the parameters Fortune used were financial. They looked at revenue growth, stock price, and all the key financial metrics. We discussed it and decided not to actively promote

the award. The choice was simple—that's not what we're focusing on every day; it's not what's driving our employees day in and day out. The award didn't emphasize our mission, which is to improve the lives of patients. Of course, as a public company, you have to generate shareholder value, but at the end of the day, we focus on helping patients, doing the right thing, and being a great place to work. And we believe that if we focus on those goals and live our values every day, the financial performance will come. Not that we haven't had ups and downs through the years, but maintaining our focus has led to the financial performances that Fortune recognized.

Coming from the toxic, numbers-at-all-costs corporate environment of Healthsouth in the 1980s and '90s, I find Eric's comments enlightening. Words like *focus* and *goals* were used plenty by Richard Scrushy in our hellish Monday morning meetings, but he was talking only about making the quarterly Wall Street estimates. We rarely heard words like *doing the right thing* or *values* or *mission* during those days. If we did, it was in some media interview or at a ground-breaking ceremony for the latest library or school building with Richard's name on it.

Values Define the Company

Starting in the 1980s, an onslaught of popular business books became available by authors like Robert Townsend, Warren Bennis, Tom Peters, Spencer Johnson, Peter Drucker, and others. Many of these books talked about the importance of mission and values in an organization. The two words often get tangled together on websites, but the way I look at it is that a mission is the reason the business exists—what it does. The company's values define what's at the heart of the business—how it undertakes its mission. A numbers-only business culture gives short shrift to such words because making money is

ETHICAL PLAY #21

"Surround financial goals with ethics."

If a company's culture seems to be that of only "making the numbers," employees will get the message and emulate the behavior of top management to be held in a favorable light.

To protect employees from bending the rules to meet their financial goals, management must put goals in an ethical framework and communicate it clearly.

their mission without valuing much else.

To me, an organization is defined more by its values than its mission. For instance, some national used car companies have popped up in the last few years in a landscape of smaller, locally-owned car lots. These megastores realized that they could sell more cars if they do three things consistently: maintain a large vehicle inventory, remove the buying pressure from the customer and post a no-haggle, lowest-possible price on the car—and stick with it. Any car dealer can say that their mission is to sell cars, or even sell them at the lowest possible price. But these national outfits, many of them very successful, communicate what they value—a friendly, no-pressure/no-negotiation environment—by their very business model.

I'm not necessarily holding these companies up as models of good ethical behavior, but they do seem to have a good handle at integrating *mission* and *values*. Can your business learn a lesson from them?

Living Your Values

Integrating values into an organization takes time and a lot of work. These values need to be constantly communicated, so the words you use need to be short and memorable. They need to be authentic and, if they are to stick, they need to be used consistently throughout the organization. This effort may start at the top, but a leader has to hire people who honestly buy into those values, even becoming evangelists for them, within the company. Bruce Cozadd seems to have found such a person in Eric Fink.

Eric explained that Bruce and a few others started the company in 2003 with two big ideas in mind: to add value to patients' lives and to be a best place to work.

What's refreshing to me is that here we are 11 years later, and we're still focusing on the same ideas. If you walk into any of our offices, you won't find our values posted on the wall anywhere. That's very deliberate, because it's not about them being posted so that people can recite them or others can see them. It's about living them every day. I see us consistently making decisions throughout the years that align with those values.

Starts at the Top

How do you build the kind of company culture that attracts great talent, trains them in the firm's values, and keeps them aligned with those values—getting great performance from them in the meantime?

It almost always has to start at the top.

Leadership plays a big part in the ethical muscle of an organization. It sets the tone. If a leader leads with integrity, values something beyond profits, and empowers those in the company to live out their values day to day, chances are good that ethical lapses will be few, employee quality of life will be better, and the company will prosper.

The Flip Side of the Leadership/Culture Equation

Just as the ethical behavior in a company culture is affected by the tone at the top, our nation's ethical behavior is powerfully impacted by *its* leaders.

The list includes political leaders, church officials, teachers, military leaders, movie stars, and athletes. In large part, because of Internet technology and massive PR efforts, we are exposed to these people a hundred times each day. Their behavior, decisions, and attitudes are certain to have some impact on our behavior and, in some ways, we are responsible for their actions.

Think about movie stars and athletes. Because of our fondness for these people, they are able to earn millions of dollars each year. We reward them greatly for who they are and what they do. Oddly, in some cases they really do not have much talent, just lots of star power. The Kardashian phenomenon just baffles me. Congress as an institution has a public approval rating in the single digits—yet we seem to keep electing the same bunch. Reality TV shows are filled with despicable people doing questionable things for their 15 minutes of fame. Athletes who publicly behave very badly are paid millions. Even some Heisman Trophy winners can't stay out of trouble off the field.

Paying and praising these people so lavishly creates conflict of interest for these people, often resulting in unethical behavior.

For example, in sports we want to believe our athletes and coaches do not cheat to win. But the rewards for winning are great. Cheating happens. Fans could even turn a blind eye to it if it benefited their teams.

For years, some college football players have been paid to play. On the ESPN show *30-30*, Coach Barry Switzer admitted that the University of Oklahoma paid Marcus Dupree, considered by many to be the most talented football player to ever come out of high school, to play for Oklahoma. When Dupree was asked what he wanted, he said he wished for a new mobile home for his mother. Within a week a new mobile home was delivered to her lot. I'm not sure, but maybe Coach Switzer rationalized his actions as helping a needy lady and making thousands of University of Oklahoma fans very happy. Ironically, Barry Switzer was inducted into to the College Football Hall of Fame in 2002.

This kind of behavior does not bring out the best in the rest of us. Unfortunately, young people, who are online 24/7, are exposed to bad behavior at every turn. It's no wonder Marianne Jennings says that only about a third of her graduate students start the school term with some sense of ethical behavior and responsibility!

In the business setting, how do we counter a culture in which honorable actions aren't honored and misbehavior is just business as usual? Once a company has leadership that values strong ethics, how do you communicate that throughout the organization and beyond?

CHAPTER 22

Ethical Reminders

Some companies are not founded with an intentional, values-driven culture. For organizations that are moving toward this way of thinking and doing business, Dr. Ariely suggests that our willingness and tendency to cheat could be diminished if we are given reminders of ethical standards. The good news from his research is that people seem to *want* to be honest, which suggests that it might be wise to incorporate moral reminders into situations that tempt us to be dishonest.

Hiring and Training with Values

Jazz Pharmaceuticals is careful when hiring to make sure there's a cultural fit between company and candidate. They do this by exposing the candidate to an assortment of Jazz employees, some of whom might ask questions about how the candidate handled a particular situation to measure attitudes toward important company values, such as integrity and collaboration.

At its twice-monthly new hire classes, the HR team gives each new employee a "values blueprint" to introduce Jazz's emphasis on its core values: collaboration, pursuit of excellence, passion, innovation, and integrity. Eric Fink explains.

> The values blueprint is four to five bullet points that describe what "good" looks like and what our expectations are at Jazz. When all new hires start, we give them that blueprint. What's brilliant about it is that right there, from day one, all new employees hear that in our performance system, collaboration, for instance, is just as important

as achieving your goal. It also gives employees a sense of what they can expect as they begin to collaborate with colleagues around the globe and what those colleagues will be expecting of them.

Pharmaceutical companies work in a very complex regulatory space. With hundreds of employees, how does Jazz help its people avoid the ethical landmines?

When we do product training, we ensure that we're highlighting our values in that training, including how to demonstrate integrity and how to interact ethically with healthcare professionals. For manager and leadership development, we focus on developing a manager's ability to have coaching conversations about our values, as well as about performance against goals. How do employees keep our values alive? How do managers emphasize the importance of those values within their groups?

As important as it is for upper management to model and speak to company values from the top, I think the key to success is to weave them into everything you do, which means you have to bake them into your on-boarding and into all of your ongoing training.

Honor Code

Sarah Polhill talked about the benefits of having ethical reminders at school, which helps everyone stay focused on the values that the Altamont community holds in common.

I think one of the best things about Altamont is the honor code. The honor code isn't just a little thing that hangs up on the wall. It does hang up in all areas of our school, but it is really supported and talked about by our teachers.

Even if a student comes in not really with that reinforced

conscience of what is right and wrong as far as academic ethics, it is part of the overall culture of the school. So if they're thinking of cheating or planning on cheating, there is that hesitation that they feel because of the way that Altamont prioritizes honor in their environment.

Sarah mentioned that, while her fellow students' moral upbringing depends on their family, when they come to Altamont it is definitely clear what the school believes and stands for. But how is that communicated?

The honor code and the honor court are talked about frequently. That way, students are aware of the consequences and how seriously we take it. Every test we have, we sign an honor pledge, and often a teacher won't even accept the test if you haven't done that. Your fellow students often will remind you. If someone is thinking of cheating, there will always be students around (who will speak up).

This culture of integrity can't be separated from the school itself. It's exhibited in everything the students say and do. What these students absorb at Altamont will, I'm sure, follow them through college and throughout their careers.

What can business learn from the Altamont School?

Ethics Pledge

Cuyahoga County, Ohio, which includes the city of Cleveland, was embroiled in a scandal over payoffs to corrupt politicians. In 2008, dozens of federal agents raided homes and offices of public officials and business owners. Sixty-two people were charged with corruption and 47 were sent to prison.

In the wake of the scandal, voters changed the way county government operated. Putting wrongdoers in prison and spreading power around wasn't enough. The corrupt culture had also created a culture of silence. Headed by officials from

ETHICAL PLAY #22

"Integrity should be stressed during employee orientation."

I believe an ethics message should be delivered to an employee on his first day at work and expounded upon during orientation. It will set the right tone for his employment.

Recently, the dean of LSU's MBA program asked me to be the first speaker the students would hear in the classroom as they began their two-year course. He wanted the students to know, right out of the box, that ethics training would be an important part of the MBA program. I was honored to deliver that message.

the Cleveland Clinic, business leaders formed the Northeast Ohio Business Ethics Coalition. Since 2010, 907 companies—including giants like Aflac, Honeywell, and Otis Elevator—have signed its 262-word pledge rejecting corruption and unethical conduct in its business affairs and urging others to do the same. "We believe," the pledge goes, "that it is important both to speak out against such conduct and to lead by example."

It seems to be working. Former Ohio governor George Voinovich told *Business Week* magazine in a March 2013 article, "There's a sense of relief in the community that the corruption has been eliminated." Dave Roman, the Cleveland Clinic's chief legal officer, said in the same article, "It's very clear that there's a good feeling about how the government is working, certainly on the ethics."

Awards and Accolades

It can't hurt for companies to be recognized by their peers, the media or industry groups for efforts in ethics and corporate social responsibility.

Business Ethics magazine, first published in 1982, gives annual awards to companies leading the way ethically. *Forbes* produces an annual list of most ethical companies. Universities are starting to recognize ethically strong companies. For instance, University of Colorado's business school issues the Leeds Summit Award each year to companies that leverage social initiatives or environmental leadership in their business practices. Kimberly-Clark Corporation was recently awarded the Most Ethical Company by the Ethisphere Institute for the third year in a row.

Survey for Cultural Improvement

Taking the temperature of employees' thoughts and reactions—and acting on the results—can improve a company's ethical environment. Twice a year, Jazz performs a qualitative survey through one-on-one interviews, focus groups, and discussions with employees. What do they learn from these employees? They learn why they're there, what they like about Jazz, what Jazz is doing well, and what it can do better.

Each November, Eric rolls out the annual engagement survey, which dives into engagement and alignment around the company's mission, values, and culture. "We're fully transparent," said Fink. "It's anonymous. We report all the results back, and in January we'll make commitments at the "All That Jazz" meeting (the company-wide quarterly videoconference) as to where we're going to invest and improve as an organization over the coming year."

From the look of it, Jazz employees are happy to be there. Fink tells us why.

> At the end of 2013, over 93% of our employees said they were aligned with our mission and that *that* drove them and was an important reason why they're at the company. In the qualitative survey, we asked, "Why are you here?" Typically, when you ask that question in employee surveys, the answers come down to job title, pay, and incentives. Those are in our list, but they're not at the top of employee priorities. What comes up first is, "I feel like I'm contributing to a bigger cause," "I believe in the mission," "I believe in the values of our company." I think that alignment is a key to our success in retaining talent. It's also been key to attracting talent.

Reinforcing Culture in Performance Reviews

Most performance review processes ask the question, "Did an employee achieve his or her goals?" When Jazz looks at employee performance, goal achievement is only half the picture.

We redesigned the employee performance review process several years ago to focus on both the *what* and the *how*. The *what* involves whether you meet your goals, but equally important how you meet them. All employees are rated by their peers and manager on how they perform and how they model the values of the organization day in and day out. Performance at Jazz is performing on both of those variables. And, because it ties back to ethics, integrity in job performance is critical; how we treat each other, how we represent the patients, and how we represent our business. Do we live up to commitments? Are we truthful?

Reminding employees of their ethical responsibilities only makes sense. A poster in the break room or a motivational speaker once a year won't do it. Whatever you use in your company has to be authentic to your stated values—and reinforce the culture you are trying to build—or employees will dismiss it as phony. It needs to be "baked" into the company culture so everybody gets the message all the time in many different ways. We're humans; we tend to forget things if they are not a priority.

It's possible that ethical reminders will help employees see less grey and more black and white. That means fewer rationalizations that can lead to ethical breaches.

CHAPTER 23

Ethics Education

Today, universities play a big role in advancing ethical business behavior, but this was not always the case. As a business student in college during the 1960s, I do not recall any course, or segment of a course, dealing with ethical issues. Universities now use many ethics textbooks, and some colleges have degree programs built around ethics, compliance, and corporate social responsibility.

The scholars who teach ethics have several major professional associations, including:

- Social Issues in Management division of the Academy of Management
- Organization and Natural Environment division of the Academy of Management
- Society for Business Ethics
- International Society for Business and Society
- European Business Ethics Network

These and other organizations publish:

- *Business & Society*
- *Business Ethics Quarterly*
- *Journal of Business Ethics*
- *Business and Professional Ethics*
- *Business and Society Review*
- *Business Ethics*
- *Academy of Management Review*
- *California Management Review*

- *Academy of Management Executive*
- *Harvard Business Review*

Menlo College

Since 2009, I have spoken at 70 different universities and have met hundreds of students. It has been a great learning experience interacting with a variety of leading ethics professors and outstanding young adults. One particular school that stands out for me is Menlo College in Atherton, California, known as "Silicon Valley's business school."

When I made my first visit to Menlo in 2010, a student picked me up at the airport and drove me to the campus. During the drive I asked him how many students attended the college. He said about 800. I jokingly asked him what kind of season the football team was having (thinking it would be too small to support a team). He replied, "We are having a very good season!" He said sports programs were a big part of being a Menlo student. The men have baseball, basketball, golf, soccer, and wrestling teams. The women have basketball, soccer, softball, volleyball, wrestling, and golf teams. About 75% of the students are involved in athletics. The school recruits outstanding high school students, many of whom want to continue competing in sports as they pursue their business degree. The students study multiple aspects of business, with many majoring in accounting and sports management.

The professor who invited me to speak at Menlo was Dr. Leslie Sekerka. Dr. Sekerka earned a Ph.D. in organizational behavior from Case Western Reserve University. She is the founding director of the Ethics in Action Research and Education Center at Menlo. Her teaching is influenced by her ongoing research in adult moral development. When she finished her doctorate and was preparing to graduate, she realized she knew only a little about the actual study of philosophy itself. This prompted her to pursue additional education and

ETHICAL PLAY #23

"Finishing without baggage is the goal."

You can spend a lifetime doing things ethically and building a legacy of respect, but one major transgression can change that legacy forever. I will not be remembered as a person who helped build one of the largest companies in Alabama history. I will be remembered as the man who helped cook HealthSouth's books.

research, exploring how philosophy actually relates to ethical decision-making and moral action in the workplace.

I find Dr. Sekerka to be a no-nonsense teacher. She is very good at challenging her students to speak up, even when they may not be eager to think about ethics in business. Just before I spoke to her first class, she warned me that a student had recently been caught cheating. He was going to apologize to the class, recognizing that his actions had impacted them, and would then introduce me as the day's guest speaker. I must say it made me more acutely aware that my talk that day was serious business.

The young man has since graduated from Menlo and, like many of her students, has been in touch with Dr. Sekerka. She told me one of the great rewards of teaching is that many of her former students reconnect to tell her that what they learned at Menlo has helped them deal with difficult ethical situations as they pursue their business careers.

Dr. Linda Treviño

In 1995, Dr. Linda Treviño co-authored a textbook with Katherine Nelson called *Managing Business Ethics: Straight Talk About How to Do It Right*, published by John Wiley. Now in its sixth edition, it is widely used in universities across the U.S. and beyond. When she started at Penn State there was not a social scientific field of study in business ethics, so she relied on her own research and taught ethics within her organizational behavior class.

I asked Dr. Treviño about the emergence of ethics-related education over the past few years. Here's what she said.

> I think that Enron, WorldCom, HealthSouth, all of those implosions, did contribute to an understanding that, "Gee, something is wrong here, there is a problem here that we need to understand better." Look at all these people who

went to the very top business schools. You know, business schools are somewhat responsible for what happened. It seemed clear that by the time of the subprime debacle [the need for increased ethics education and awareness] was already pretty well developed and that just, you know, helped to confirm what people already thought.

Dr. Treviño is director of the Shoemaker Program in Business Ethics, originally endowed by Mr. and Mrs. G. Albert Shoemaker because of the importance with which they regarded ethics in corporate conduct. The centerpiece of the program is the Shoemaker Lecture, which brings speakers to campus to talk with students.

She continues to do research in the field of ethics and takes great pride in knowing that she has contributed knowledge to this area of business education.

The Corporate Connection

Several universities have developed outreach business ethics centers, including the Darden School at the University of Virginia, the Wharton School at Penn State, and Duquesne University. These centers offer ethics training programs to help companies develop codes of conduct.

At Bentley University in Waltham, Massachusetts, the Center for Business Ethics provides a five-day executive development course in partnership with the Ethics and Compliance Officer Association. The course, "Managing Ethics in Organizations," was the first of its kind to provide ethics and compliance practitioners with a professional credential along with practical knowledge to manage an organization's efforts to ensure business integrity.

At Silicon Valley's Santa Clara University, the Markkula Center for Applied Ethics offers an executive education course along with publications, debates, and courses in business ethics, bioethics, campus ethics, character education, government ethics, and Internet ethics. At Ethics Camp, K-12 teachers learn to integrate character education into their curricula.

Let the Sunshine In

One of the main tenets of business ethics education is transparency, the intentional sharing of information by a company with stakeholders and the public. "Let the sunshine in" has new meaning for companies that are trying to build a more open, ethical business culture.

CHAPTER 24

Business Transparency

Building in transparency is a vital part of becoming an ethical company. The act of being transparent takes honesty to a whole new level. Today, consumers have a far wider range of information about business practices than five decades ago. Think about these examples:

- Nutritional content of foods is now exposed to buyer view.
- Ratios of males to females in jobs, along with their pay scales, are calculated and published by the government.
- Sky-high executive salaries, bonuses, and perks are leaked in the media and online.
- Crash-worthiness of cars and SUVs is widely available in magazines and the Internet.

As customers, stockholders, and employees, we don't want to know everything about a company. We just want to know the parts that affect us. When a company is perceived to be hiding something—ingredients, negative product research, medication side effects, financial performance, you name it—we become wary of their motives and lose trust in them.

An article in the *Journal of Management* says, "Corporate transparency describes the extent to which a corporation's actions are observable by outsiders. This is a consequence of regulation, local norms, and the set of information, privacy, and business policies concerning corporate decision making and operations openness to employees, stakeholders, shareholders and the general public. From the perspective of outsiders, transparency can be defined simply as the perceived quality of intentionally shared information from the corporation."

Why It's So Important

Why is transparency so important in business at this moment? It's a business builder—or a business killer.

Living in an era when personal and corporate secrets can be unraveled with a few lines of code or clicks of the mouse, it is only a matter of time before the public discovers the facts. Given that false information and accusations—not to mention the truth—can travel at light speed via the Internet, corporate reputations are at stake.

Many companies have committed to being more transparent in their operations and communications. Doing so is clearly in their best interests. It is one thing for a company to tell its story through media coverage or advertising, but the most powerful impact, according to a recent article in *The Guardian*, is when a company is confident enough in its process or operations to bring viewers in to see exactly how things are done. It is the ultimate in show and tell.

Transparency in Action

In this age of instant YouTube videos and social media sharing, there are many examples of companies "coming clean" with the public to gain its favor. In fact, the social media company Buffer recently revealed their pay structure—right down to the CEO's salary—in a blog post. The company was then inundated with resumes.

CEO Jim Whitehurst of the software company Red Hat has an employee-fueled forum called "memo-list," which functions as a social network to facilitate communication about major issues or any other topic that should be openly discussed. Jim and other leaders interact, encouraging collaboration and transparency in decision-making.

When AT&T had a fiber cut in the San Francisco Bay Area, they turned to Twitter to get the word out about the issue, then had multiple Tweets even if there was no update so that their 2400 followers knew exactly what was going on. They now have over 20,000 Twitter followers.

Transparency is something that a company mostly controls and that mostly reassures its customers. By giving people a window into its workings, a company can show it has a sound process to which it's adhering. It can avoid asking customers to have faith in a black box. The greater the transparency, in other words, the greater the trust.

But not every company wants to let the sunshine in, so government and nonprofit watchdog groups have had to step in. Today there are countless government agencies from local to federal to international that are designed to enforce transparency so that consumers, investors, and society at large can be protected against unethical behavior.

Compliance Enforcement

Regulations are needed to enforce corporate transparency, but do we pass more and more laws and give longer prison terms for those violating them? There is evidence that this does not work well—it is also very expensive. Every time a new federal law such Sarbanes-Oxley or Dodd-Frank is passed, government workers have to be hired to administer and enforce these laws. When Dodd-Frank was passed in 2010, almost 2,600 federal employees were added with a budget of $3 billion for a five-year period.

Costs increase for companies that have to deal with these new laws. In 1997 when I left HealthSouth, I was just beginning to hear that public companies were adding corporate compliance officers. It seemed that with all of the laws concerning sexual harassment, the environment, race and age discrimination—and the financial fraud potential companies had to address—it was time for oversight by an officer-level employee.

The cost of investigating and prosecuting crimes and incarcerating the guilty is very large. It is estimated that it costs the federal government $21,000 a year to house a prisoner. During the incarceration, the prisoner pays no taxes and his family may require government assistance.

Technology and Transparency

Probably more than any one thing, the Internet helps encourage business transparency. Today we are electronically interconnected with people all over the world. We are sharing, collaborating, publishing, critiquing, helping, learning, competing, and having fun in ways impossible 20 years ago. (Before my first grandchild was 15 minutes old, I was sending pictures of him all over the country. Within ten minutes my family and friends were responding. Of course, they all commented on how good looking he was.)

In 2008, Zuckerberg's Law emerged. Facebook founder Mark Zuckerberg said, "I would expect that next year, people would be sharing twice as much information as they shared this year. And next year, they will be sharing twice as much as they did the year before."

Will this exponential increase in information sharing continue to make business people behave with more transparency, and, by extension, more ethically?

I hope it does. After all, I want to believe that the Internet is good for other things besides cat videos.

Transparency in Healthcare

Our nation's health insurance industry is poised for improvement through greater transparency. As it is now, most customers do not trust the industry. It doesn't communicate well with its customers. Consumers just don't understand the system and

ETHICAL PLAY #24

"Be skeptical of philanthropy."

Just as politicians can be influenced by lobbyists, society can be influenced by the philanthropy from business people. Corporations often try to buy public goodwill by being philanthropic. A company may do good, but that doesn't necessarily make it a good company.

in particular, how healthcare is priced. It is very difficult if not impossible to understand the statement of costs you receive from the hospital after just a three-day stay.

As a child, I remember my mother taking me to see the family doctor when I needed medical care. It was very simple. It was the doctor and his nurse—no insurance company or middleman was between our family and the physician. By the time I was graduating from college in 1967, I could see the change coming. Students were beginning to talk about working for companies that offered healthcare insurance. Employer-sponsored health insurance plans began surging during World War II. Federally-imposed wage controls prohibited employers from raising wages enough to attract workers, but there were no limits on fringe benefits such as health insurance. That started the trend that is now an expected part of an employee's compensation package. It is interesting to note that, originally, it was not something workers were demanding—it was provided to them in lieu of higher wages.

This, of course, set into motion a system for purchasing healthcare that my mother could never have imagined. You now had an entity between the consumer and the actual provider of healthcare. The insurance company was a middleman but was actually paying the bills. Over time the person paying the bills begins to call the shots. He will dictate the pricing and access. In the case of Medicare, the government is the middleman and the government calls the shots.

The Big Problem

The big problem with this system is that over time the healthcare providers and the healthcare consumers have no control. They don't know what is going on. The insurance companies like it this way.

In healthcare, unlike other industries, pricing for healthcare can vary dramatically, depending on who's paying. Princeton economist Ume Reinhardt likens shopping for healthcare to shopping in a department store, blindfolded, and weeks later being handed a statement that says, "Pay this amount."

In a Wall Street Journal article from February 23, 2014, Melinda Beck gave examples of how hospital prices can vary hugely. The average charge for joint replacement surgery ranged from $5,300 in Ada, Oklahoma to $223,000 in Monterey Park, California. In Jackson, Mississippi, an episode of heart failure was $9,000 in one hospital and $51,000 in another. A hospital in Pennington, New Jersey, charged $3,036 for an outpatient diagnostic and screening ultrasound while one in Bronx, New York, billed just $88.

Hospitals Want Transparency

In the article, Melinda Beck quotes AHA president Rich Umbdenstock as saying that hospitals "are absolutely in favor of price transparency," and they support a bill currently in Congress that would let individual states determine price-disclosure rules. He also says hospitals would like to end the confusing pricing practices, but they can't do it without big changes in payment practices by both the government and the insurance industry.

Traditionally, the rates insurance companies negotiate with healthcare providers have been proprietary information. Insurance companies do not want the public to know what they are willing to settle for. This is unethical. It may be legal but it is not in the best interests of the public.

This can all be changed over time. With the explosion in technology it might not be a very long time. The technology is here now. There is no sound reason why we should not be able to go online and see the prices charged by hospitals in our city, state, and nation for specific procedures. The insurance industry will come up with reasons why it cannot be done, but these reasons will be bogus. With all of the emotional political debate over healthcare reform, it is amazing to me that transparency in pricing has gotten so little attention.

What about Washington, D.C.?

Comedian George Burns said, "If you can fake sincerity, you've got it made."

Nobody fakes sincerity like politicians. And when someone is fake, you know they're hiding something.

One of the most frequently-asked questions after people hear my talk, is, "What can be done about Washington?" It's interesting because I never mention politics in my talks. It's obvious there's an ethics problem there.

To get a firsthand perspective, I called my childhood friend from Bossier City, Louisiana, Buddy Roemer. Buddy was the 52nd Governor of Louisiana from 1988 to 1992 and previously served in the U.S. House of Representatives from 1981 to 1988. He was also a candidate for the presidential nomination of the Republican Party in 2012. Buddy, who is now in banking, says transparency is the first step to changing Washington.

Taking money out of the political system is impossible. But in government and politics we must have full disclosure. It should be immediate. Let the sunlight in. With the Internet this is possible. If a lady in Butte, Montana, can tell the entire world that her cat, Fluffy, had six kittens yesterday, surely full disclosure of money to politicians is possible.

Ethical Gems from Buddy

Here are some more things Buddy says should happen.

- Corporate gifts to politicians should be prohibited. Gifts should be from an individual and, of course, declared publicly.
- There should be no PACs and no super PACs. The individual giving the gifts must be an American citizen.

- Lobbyists should try to influence congressmen with ideas, not a check. A lobbyist should not be a congressman's bagman.

Buddy has an idea of how to really shake up the system. Imagine two types of candidates: the Free Speech candidates and the Citizen candidates. The Free Speech candidates could receive any amount of money from an individual as long as it was disclosed. The Citizen candidate would limit the contributions he accepted to $100—and only from people able to vote in his district. Once he received $100,000, the money would be matched five-to-one by the federal government. Then the battle lines would not be Republican vs. Democrat but the free speech candidate vs. the citizen candidate.

Better Living Through Transparency

Information is power. These days, though, it seems that we, as individuals, feel less powerful while institutions around us increase their power. More transparency in government and in the business would, without a doubt, would allow people to make better choices and solve a number of ethical ills.

CHAPTER 25

What's Next?

We've spent some time together thinking about how we can change ourselves and our business culture to become more ethical, but people do not simply change their beliefs and habits overnight. When the Surgeon General published his report on smoking in 1964, many smokers probably thought, "So what? It's my right to smoke."

Over time, education can change behavior. I use the smoking example because I was 21 years old in 1964. I had grown up with smoking as part of our social fabric. During the 1950s, more than 50% of Americans were smokers. I remember ashtrays being everywhere: gift shops, the armrests of airplanes, restaurants, and even hospitals. However, over time, I saw ashtrays disappear. I'm not sure where you can buy one today. (By the way, I wondered if there might be an ashtray museum, and there is!—the Dean Lantrip Ashtray Museum in Oroville, California. It has ashtrays from hospitals, universities, Rotary clubs, and even Presidents of the United States).

The Power of Knowledge and Pressure

By the 1970s, however, public awareness and health knowledge—combined with pressure from consumer groups and the government—caused things to change (despite intense pushback from Big Tobacco).

In 1971, Congress passed the Public Health Cigarette Smoking Act, banning the advertising of cigarettes on television and radio. Since 1982, cigarette companies have been forced to place Surgeon General warnings on all cigarette

ETHICAL PLAY #25

"It's okay to talk about ethics."

When someone asks me what I do for a living, I say I speak about ethics. Then the person will say something like, "Boy that is certainly needed." When I ask them to elaborate, they often give me an idea for my next speech.

To increase the public trust in business, we need more open conversations about ethics.

packs. These actions and others have been successful in changing our culture concerning smoking. Less than a quarter of the population smokes today, and smoking in public has decreased greatly. You can get on an airplane or check into a hotel room and it does not smell like an ashtray.

The important thing to realize is that this cultural acceptance of smoking did not start to change until it was very clear that it was a danger to our health.

Likewise, until the Enron/Tyco era and the subprime debacle, most people did not perceive unethical business behavior as a grave danger to our economic health. Now that we do, what are we going to do about it?

The Best Game Plan to Win Ethically

You may not be able to control a business culture, but you can control yourself. If I could give only one piece of advice concerning ethics, it would be to try for complete abstinence from behaving unethically. We now know about the fudge factor, and it should inspire us to behave ethically.

Every time we cheat a little, we are taking the first step on the slippery slope. What is the right amount of cheating on an expense report, padding an insurance claim, of cheating on a test? What is the right amount of insider trading, the right amount of cooking the books, the right amount of lying to your investors?

The answer to all of these questions is zero.

Of course, it is impossible to be perfect, but the playbook should ask for perfection. The best coaches ask their players to train for perfection. The goal is to make the perfect pass, make the perfect block, have the best game plan, and to win every game.

I am cautiously optimistic for the future because I know that anybody can make the choice to be ethical—and it is a choice.

The Path I Took

Every day I think about the wrong I did during my days at HealthSouth and the people who were irreparably harmed because of it. Why did I make the wrong choices?

Because, while I had some integrity, I lacked courage. I had business sense, but not a fine-tuned sense of business ethics. I had money and things, but no moral barometer telling me when enough was enough. I knew right from wrong, but there weren't many moral reminders present in my life and in my work setting to help keep me on the right path.

These aren't excuses for my past behavior, but rather some of the things that come to mind when I wonder, "If I had read an ethics playbook like this back in the day, would it have made any difference? Could it have helped me avoid the needless pain I caused myself and others?"

I'd like to think that yes, it could have helped.

Will it help you? Will it help you avoid the slippery slope that takes a good person down a bad road slowly but surely? Will it possibly inspire you to help others behave more ethically?

I hope it will.

NOTES

Chapter 1

South African entrepreneur Harold Ruttenberg developed a concept...
"Contemporary Auditing: Real Issues & Cases, Seventh Edition," by
Michael C. Knapp, 2010 Cengage Learning.

Before the end of the year, the company...
U.S. Justice Department press release, February 25, 2004 http://
www.justice.gov/opa/pr/2004/February/04_crm_110.htm.

Chapter 2

"Corporate" comes from the Latin word...
Merriam-Webster Dictionary online, http://www.merriam-webster.
com/dictionary/corporate.

In their 2014 Global Fraud Study, they focus on occupational fraud...
"Report to the Nations on Occupational Fraud and Abuse, 2014
Global Fraud Study," Association of Certified Fraud Examiners, 2014
http://www.acfe.com/rttn/docs/2014-report-to-nations.pdf.

...as of the end of 2011, various FBI field offices were pursuing...
Financial Crimes Report to the Public, Fiscal Years 2010-
2011, FBI http://www.fbi.gov/stats-services/publications/
financial-crimes-report-2010-2011.

...like when a Minnesota woman who, during...
"Church and Synagogue Security News," June 24, 2013
http://blog.congregationalsecurityinc.com/tag/embezzlement/#.
UoUGgI2E554.

Chapter 3

...when the giant ship hit a reef in Prince William Sound, Alaska...
"The Valdez," by Gregory Palast, *The Observer,* July 2005; "Software System Safety," by Nancy Levenson, *Anchorage Daily News*, March 4, 2009; "Captain of *Exxon Valdez* offers 'heartfelt apology' for oil spill," by Wesley Loy, *Anchorage Daily News*. March 4, 2009.

The 2014 edition of Webster's Dictionary defines success as...
Merriam-Webster Dictionary http://www.merriam-webster.com/ dictionary/success?show=0&t=1413762153.

Chapter 4

She quotes Dennis Kozlowski, the CEO at Tyco...
The Seven Signs of Ethical Collapse: How to Spot Moral Meltdowns in Companies Before It's Too Late, by Marianne Jennings, St. Martin's Press, 2006.

...they fail to realize that they play the role of useful idiots...
Ibid.

Marianne Jennings reminded me of a very wealthy executive...
Conversation with Marianne Jennings, 2014.

They do well in power professions like business and finance...
"The Sociopath Next Door," by Martha Stout, Harmony, 2006

Chapter 5

His 2012 book, The (Honest) Truth About Dishonesty, asks...
The (Honest) Truth About Dishonesty, by Dr. Dan Ariely, Harper Perennial Reprint Edition, 2013.

Dr. Ariely makes the case that people are more likely to commit...
Ibid.

Enablers let themselves believe that delivery of short-term results...
Blind Spots: Why We Fail to Do What's Right and What to Do About

It, by Max H. Bazerman and Ann E. Tenbrunsel, Princeton University Press, 2011.

"Here's the thing," Dan Ariely told me. *"If you think about..."*
Correspondence with Dan Ariely, 2014.

Chapter 6

The outward appearance of a great financial success can encourage...
"Report to the Nations on Occupational Fraud and Abuse, 2014
Global Fraud Study," Association of Certified Fraud Examiners, 2014
http://www.acfe.com/rttn/docs/2014-report-to-nations.pdf.

In one of my conversations with Professor Marianne Jennings, she told...
Conversation with Marianne Jennings, 2014.

Ethical Play # 6
Mistakes Were Made (But Not by Me): Why We Justify Foolish Beliefs, Bad Decisions and Hurtful Acts, by Carol Tavris and Elliot Aronson, 2007

Chapter 7

Enron's auditor, Arthur Andersen, charged consulting...
"The Fall of Enron," by Krishna Palepu, Journal of Economic Perspectives, 2003.

The Tyco board was an assemblage of Kozlowski insiders. While the...
The Seven Signs of Ethical Collapse: How to Spot Moral Meltdowns in Companies Before It's Too Late, by Marianne Jennings, St. Martin's Press, 2006.

Dr. Ariely, in one of his YouTube videos, states that bankers...
Dan Ariely YouTube video: "RSA Animate—The Truth About Dishonesty," 2012, https://www.youtube.com/watch?v=XBmJay_qdNc.

She began her career on Wall Street in 1988 and retired in 2005. It...
Correspondence with Deborah Lawson, 2014.

Tim Cook, CEO of Apple (and an Alabama native), was asked at the... "Apple CEO Tim Cook Is One Happy Dude," by Thomas Lee, Businessweek, September 22, 2014.

Chapter 8

Dr. Ariely has done research in the area of the hidden cost of favors...
The (Honest) Truth About Dishonesty, by Dan Ariely, Harper Perennial Reprint Edition, 2013.

"A lot of things are wrong in D.C. I think the first one is...
Correspondence with Dan Ariely, 2014.

Vendor fraud can be divided into two groups: fraud committed...
"Case in Point: EisnerAmper's Litigation Services Newsletter"
 http://www.eisneramper.com/litigation-Business-Valuation/detect-vendor-fraud-0512.aspx.

Chapter 9

In his book, Wall Street Values, Dr. Michael A. Santoro writes that...
Wall Street Values, by Michael A. Santoro and Ronald J. Strauss, Cambridge University Press, 2012.

By one Federal Reserve estimate, the country lost almost an entire...
"2008 Financial Crisis Impact Still Hurting States," by
Jake Grovum, USA Today, September 15, 2013 http://
www.usatoday.com/story/money/business/2013/09/14/
impact-on-states-of-2008-financial-crisis/2812691/.

The deep and persistent losses of the recession forced states to make...
Ibid.

Chapter 10

...a code that straddles the line between what investors want to hear ...
(The mandatory financial report a public company files with the SEC has a component called Management's Discussion and Analysis of Financial Condition and Results of Operations, or MD&A. The SEC's

goal for this document is for management to communicate with investors in a clear and straightforward manner that not only meets technical disclosure requirements but also is informative and transparent.) Source: "Commission Guidance Regarding Management's Discussion and Analysis of Financial Condition and Results of Operations," SEC 17 CFR Parts 211, 231 and 241, Release Nos. 33-8350; 34-48960; FR-72.

In The (Honest) Truth About Dishonesty, Dan Ariely tells about... The (Honest) Truth About Dishonesty, by Dan Ariely, Harper Perennial Reprint Edition, 2013.

An article in The New Yorker explains that Greek citizens have what... "Dodger Mania," by James Surowiecki, The New Yorker, July 11, 2011.

Dr. Max Bazerman explains that people can inherently believe their... Blind Spots: Why We Fail to Do What's Right and What to Do About It, by Max H. Bazerman and Ann E. Tenbrunsel, Princeton University Press, 2011.

Lee Ross called the "fundamental attribution error." This is the... "Ethical Decision Making: More Needed than Good Intentions," by Robert Prentice, Financial Analysts Journal, Volume 63, Number 6, 2007.

"I did a survey with them," she said, "and 87% admitted..." Conversation with Marianne Jennings, 2014.

Chapter 11

Even well-intentioned people can stumble into ethical minefields... "Ethical Decision Making: More Needed than Good Intentions," by Robert Prentice, *Financial Analysts Journal,* Volume 63, Number 6, 2007.

In the workplace, there are many common arguments or... Giving Voice to Values, by Mary C. Gentile, Yale, 2010.

Robert Prentice outlines several biases in how people see a situation... "Ethical Decision Making: More Needed than Good Intentions," by Robert Prentice, Financial Analysts Journal, Volume 63, Number 6, 2007.

Like Professor Dumbledore said in Harry Potter, "It takes a ...
Harry Potter and the Sorcerer's Stone, by J. K. Rowling, Scholastic, 1999.

Prentice notes that people often slide down a slippery slope in
tandem... "Ethical Decision Making: More Needed than Good
Intentions," by Robert Prentice, Financial Analysts Journal, Volume
63, Number 6, 2007.

...when independent thinking is trumped by pressures from superiors...
Ibid.

Many people, particularly leaders, can be so optimistic that they
make...
Ibid.

Marianne Jennings' research reveals that: 74% of us believe our
ethics... The Seven Signs of Ethical Collapse: How to Spot Moral
Meltdowns in Companies Before It's Too Late, by Marianne Jennings,
St. Martin's Press, 2006.

For instance, in the 1960s, after revelations about the harmfulness of...
"Use and effectiveness of tobacco telephone counseling and nicotine
therapy in Maine," by S. H. Swartz, T. M. Cowan, J. E. Klayman,
American Journal of Preventive Medicine, 2005.

Framing a question in two different ways can create two different... "Ethical Decision Making: More Needed than Good Intentions," by Robert
Prentice, *Financial Analysts Journal*, Volume 63, Number 6, 2007.

...to the endowment effect, the idea that when we become attached to...
"Choices, Values, and Frames," by D. Kahneman and A. Tversky,
American Psychologist, 1984.

Chapter 12

...which really drives home the point that, in just about everything
we... "A.B.C.'s of Behavioral Forensics," by Sridhar Ramamoorti,
David E. Morrison III, Joseph W. Koletar, and Kelly Richmond
Pope, John Wiley and Sons, 2013.

Chapter 13

Recently, Bruce introduced me to one of his key people, Eric Fink, the... Conversation with Eric Fink, 2014.

An article in CFO Magazine discusses "suspect accounting." In a... "The Search for Suspect Accounting," by Vincent Ryan, CFO magazine, April 8, 2014.

Indeed the accounting frauds at Enron, HealthSouth, WorldCom... "Predicting Material Accounting Misstatements," by Patricia Dechew of University of California Berkley, 2011.

One such study suggested a need for corporate governance reform... "Why Do CFOs Become Involved in Material Accounting Manipulations," Journal of Accounting and Economics, September 2010.

My students are very driven
Conversation with Marianne Jennings, 2014.

Chapter 14

Two MIT professors, for instance, conducted an auction of Boston... *Influences: The Psychology of Persuasion*, by Robert Cialdini, Harper Business, 1984.

Banks and credit card companies are currently mailing out over five... *Predictably Irrational*, by Dan Ariely, Harper Perennial, 2009.

Chapter 15

The first eye-opening statement in her book is that one in 25 people... *The Sociopath Next Door*, by Martha Stout, Harmony, 2006.

"It is not that this group fails to grasp the difference between good... Ibid.

The sociopath may be very intelligent and ambitious with a desire to... Ibid.

"Sociopaths are basically the perfect economic animals, right?" Correspondence with Dan Ariely, 2014.

In Snakes in Suits, Dr. Paul Babiak and Dr. Robert Hare suggest that... Snakes in Suits, by Paul Babiak and Robert Hare, HarperCollins, 2006.

"I tell them there's three components (to understanding ethical ...) Conversation with Marianne Jennings, 2014.

Chapter 16

The Altamont experience encourages students to think... Altamont School website, http://www.altamontschool.org/.

"When students come forward and turn themselves in or are... Interview with Sarah Polhill, 2014.

...confronts what she calls, "60 years of moral relativism," in... Conversation with Marianne Jennings, 2014.

Guinn wanted to do something at the high school level to recognize... Conversation with Guinn Massey, 2014.

Chapter 17

...explains that voicing your values is a competency that can be learned... Giving Voice to Values, by Mary C. Gentile, Yale, 2010.

On January 15, 2009, Captain Sullenberger landed US Airways Flight... Highest Duty: My Search for What Really Matters, by Chesley B. Sullenberger and Jeffrey Zaslow, William Morrow, 2009.

"One way of looking at this might be that for 42 years, I've been..." Chesley Sullenberger, "60 Minutes," CBS Television, 2009.

As Dr. Ariely points out, virtually all humans have the capacity to... The (Honest) Truth About Dishonesty, by Dan Ariely, Harper Perennial Reprint Edition, 2013.

"I think that anybody has choice no matter what the situations…
Interview with Sarah Polhill, 2014.

…a way to determine "the right thing" in what we say…
Rotary website, https://www.rotary.org/en/guiding-principles.

"One of the major things I've learned, especially serving on the honor…" Interview with Sarah Polhill, 2014.

If you can keep your head when all about you…
-"If," by Rudyard Kipling, *Rewards and Fairies*, 1910.

I think the secret is what Professor Jennings calls eternal vigilance…
Conversation with Marianne Jennings, 2014.

Robert Prentice says that more people accidentally back into ethical… "Ethical Decision Making: More Needed than Good Intentions," by Robert Prentice, Financial Analysts Journal, Volume 63, Number 6, 2007.

Prentice claims, and I agree, that, "Simply thinking about such ethical…"
Ibid.

Chapter 18

"I see this in my classes, too, about a third have a very strong sense…"
Conversation with Marianne Jennings, 2014.

…he argues that the Golden Rule is much more than simply an ethical…
"The Concept of Morals," by Walter Terence, McMillian, 1937.

Variations of the Rule are found in a wide range of world cultures…
"How Good People Make Tough Choices: Resolving the Dilemmas of Ethical Living," by Rushworth Kidder, Harper's Magazine, 2003.

"We want people to realize the consequences of their actions, to…"
Correspondence with Dan Ariely, 2014.

"The other thing is you want to have it (the goal of more ethical living)…"
Ibid.

Chapter 19

"I had been screened by HR and it was time for my interview with the..."
Conversation with Greg Womble, 2014.

"When you're interviewing with a company, what are the signs in the..." Conversation with Marianne Jennings, 2014.

...allows him to help drive employee engagement throughout the ...
Conversation with Eric Fink, 2014.

Dr. David Larcker at Stanford's graduate School of Business has been...
"Financial Manipulation: Words Don't Lie," by David F. Larcker and Brian Tayan, Stanford Closer Look Series, July 23, 2010.

In the call, just months before Lehman's collapse, she used the...
"The Fall of a Wall Street Highflier," by Patricia Sellers, Fortune, March 22, 2010.

Chapter 20

"There's no such thing as a perfect company because as long as humans..."
Conversation with Marianne Jennings, 2014.

...tips from whistleblowers accounted for 40% of the detections of...
"Report to the Nations on Occupational Fraud and Abuse, 2014 Global Fraud Study," Association of Certified Fraud Examiners, 2014
http://www.acfe.com/rttn/docs/2014-report-to-nations.pdf.

Approach your immediate manager first. You should find out...
Managing Business Ethics: Straight Talk about How to Do It Right, by Linda Trevino, Wiley, 2013.

You could be socially ostracized or lose your job. Even if you leave...
Whistleblowers: Incentives, Disincentives and Protection Strategies, by Fredrick D. Lipman, John Wiley and Sons, 2012.

There is a long history of financially rewarding some whistleblowers...
Ibid.

...under a qui tam action...
(In common law, a writ of *qui tam* is a writ whereby a private individual who assists a prosecution can receive all or part of any penalty imposed.) Source: http://en.wikipedia.org/wiki/Qui_tam.

However, with the median whistleblower award at only $150,000 after... Whistleblowers: Incentives, Disincentives and Protection Strategies, by Fredrick D. Lipman, John Wiley and Sons, 2012.

Chapter 21

Legend has it that a bookkeeper was denied a $100 monthly raise... "Why Employees Commit Fraud," by Joseph T. Wells, Journal of Accountancy, February 2001, American Institute of Public Accountants.

Over 30 years ago, a Hollinger and Clark study of 12,000 employees in... Ibid.

"Interestingly," said Eric Fink, "when we found out about the award... Conversation with Eric Fink, 2014.

On the ESPN show 30-30, Coach Barry Switzer admitted that the... "30-30," About the Best that Never Was, ESPN.

Chapter 22

Dr. Ariely suggests that our willingness and tendency to cheat could... The (Honest) Truth About Dishonesty, by Dan Ariely, Harper Perennial Reprint Edition, 2013.

At the twice-monthly new hire classes, Erick Fink and his team give... Conversation with Eric Fink, 2014.

"When we do product training, we ensure that we're highlighting..." Ibid.

"I think one of the best things about Altamont's honor is the honor..." Interview with Sarah Polhill, 2014.

Cuyahoga County, Ohio, which includes Cleveland, was embroiled in a...
Blind Spots: Why We Fail to Do What's Right and What to Do About It, by Max H. Bazerman and Ann E. Tenbrunsel, Princeton University Press, 2011; "Cleveland Area Companies Sign Anti-Corruption Pledge," by Mark Niquette, Businessweek, March 14, 2013.

Kimberly-Clark Corporation was recently awarded the Most Ethical...
"The World's Most Ethical Companies-Honorees," 2014 Ethisphere Magazine, http://ethisphere.com/worlds-most-ethical/wme-honorees/.

Each November, Eric rolls out their annual engagement survey, which... Conversation with Eric Fink, 2014.

"We redesigned the employee performance review process to focus..." Ibid.

Chapter 23

...corporate social responsibility ...
(Corporate Social Responsibility is a management concept whereby companies integrate social and environmental concerns in their business operations and interactions with their stakeholders. CSR is generally understood as being the way through which a company achieves a balance of economic, environmental and, social imperatives—"Triple-Bottom-Line-Approach"—while at the same time addressing the expectations of shareholders and stakeholders.)

Source: United Nations Industrial Development Organization http://www.unido.org/en/what-we-do/trade/csr/what-is-csr.html.

Dr. Sekerka earned a Ph.D. in organizational behavior from Case...
Ethics in Action Research and Education Center website http://www.sekerkaethicsinaction.com/.

"I think that Enron, WorldCom, HealthSouth, all of those implosions..." Conversation with Linda Trevino, 2014.

...the Center for Business Ethics provides a five-day executive...
Bentley University, Center for Business Ethics website http://www.

bentley.edu/centers/center-for-business-ethics.

...the Markkula Center for Applied Ethics offers an executive education... Santa Clara University, Markkula Center for Applied Ethics website http://www.scu.edu/ethics/.

Chapter 24

Nutritional content of foods is now exposed to buyer... "Corporation, Be Good! The Story of Corporate Social Responsibility," by William C. Frederick, Dog Ear Publishing, 2006.

"Corporate transparency describes the extent to which..." "Organizational Transparency: A New Perspective on Managing Trust in Organization-Stakeholder Relationships," by A. Schnackenberg, and E. Tomlinson, Journal of Management, 2014.

It is one thing for a company to tell its story through media coverage or... "Why Transparency and Authenticity Wins in Business and in Marketing," by Scott Monty, The Guardian, February 17, 2014 http://www.theguardian.com/technology/2014/feb/17/why-transparency-and-authenticity-wins-in-business-and-in-marketing.

...the social media company Buffer recently revealed their pay... Ibid.

CEO Jim Whitehurst of the software company Red Hat has an... "10 Leaders Who Aren't Afraid To Be Transparent," by John Hall, Forbes August 27, 2012.

When AT&T had a fiber cut in the San Francisco Bay Area, they turned... "Five Examples of How Being Transparent Is Good for Business," by Janine Popick, Vertical Response, January 14, 2010 http://www.verticalresponse.com/blog/5-examples-of-how-being-transparent-can-help-your-business/.

Transparency is something that a company mostly controls and that... "Trust in the Age of Transparency," by Julia Kirby, Harvard Business Review, July–August 2012 http://hbr.org/2012/07/

trust-in-the-age-of-transparency/ar/1.

Every time a new federal law such Sarbanes-Oxley or Dodd Frank is...
"Failing to End 'Too Big to Fail': An Assessment of the Dodd-Frank Act Four Years Later," by the Republican staff of the Committee on Financial Services, U.S. House of Representatives Jeb Hensarling, Chairman, July 2014.

It is estimated that it costs the federal government $21,000 a year...
"11 Facts about America's Prison Population," by Ezra Klein and Evan Soltas, The Washington Post, August 13, 2013.

"I would expect that next year, people would be sharing twice as much..." "Zuckerberg's Law of Information Sharing," by Saul Hansell, nytimes.com, November 6, 2008 http://bits.blogs.nytimes.com/2008/11/06/zuckerbergs-law-of-information-sharing/?_php=true&_type=blogs&_r=0.

Employer-sponsored health insurance plans began surging during...
"Employer-Sponsored Health Insurance and the Promise of Health Insurance Reform," by Thomas C. Buchmueller and Alan C. Monheit, The National Bureau of Economic Research, Summer 2009.

The average charge for joint replacement surgery ranged from...
"How to Bring the Price of Health Care into the Open," by Melinda Beck, Wall Street Journal, February 23, 2014.

Buddy, who is now in banking, says transparency is the first step to ...
Conversation with Buddy Roemer, 2014.

Chapter 25

...the Dean Lantrip Ashtray Museum in Oroville, California.
"Lantrip Ashtray Museum Grand Opening," The Digger Shoppe Rand News, Online Edition, August 7, 2014.

AVAILABLE AT AARONBEAM.NET: